The Creative Process

Awakening Inspiration for Art, Work, Love and Life!

by Karen McChrystal, M.A.

Warm Springs Press

The Creative Process: Awakening Inspiration for Art, Work, Love and Life!

Copyright © 1980, revised 2013, 2016, by Karen McChrystal, M.A. Originally written as Master's Thesis, for degree in Clinical Psychology.

ISBN: 978-0-9973842-1-5

Warm Springs Press
Tucson, Arizona

Printed in the United States of America

Contents

In the laboratories of individual creativity, a revolutionary alchemy transmutes the basest metals of everyday life into gold. First and foremost, the problem is to dissolve the consciousness of constraints – that is, the feeling of impotence – in the magnetic exercise of creativity; melt them in the surge of creative power, in the serene affirmation of its genius. Megalomania, sterile on the level of prestige and the spectacle, represents in this context an important stage in the struggle opposing the ego to the coalesced forces of conditioning.

Today, nihilism reigns triumphant, and in its night the spark of creativity, which is the spark of all real life, shines only the more brightly. And while the project of a superior organization of survival proves abortive, there is, as these sparks become more frequent and gradually dissolve into a single light, the promise of a new organization, based this time on a harmony of individual wills. Historic becoming has taken us to the crossing point where radical subjectivity is confronted with the possibility of transforming the world. This privileged moment is the reversal of perspective.

Treatise on Living for the Young Generation
~ Raoul Vaneigem

Prologue

"Those not busy being born are busy dying."

~Bob Dylan

Creativity is the very essence of life. Whatever your occupation, whether or not it's within the arts, what is important for anyone's vitality to keep alive the creative spirit and inspiration. It is this that keeps us from succumbing to conditioning, to conventions that don't suit us and are stifling. Depression, so widespread in our culture, often results from individuals stifling their creative spirit, and instead conforming to society in ways that do not support their inherent natures.

To live lives of inspiration, we need to understand how and whence inspiration comes. Each of us has the capacity to receive inspiration, to express our unique gifts, to express our contribution in a way that may not have been done before. This is creativity in its multi-faced form. Our innate creativity comes forth once we identify what we passionately care about, and then develop a vehicle for its expression. This can take many forms: writing, fine art, music, craftsmanship, teaching, homemaking, running a business, and even the art of relationship, statesmanship, or visionary reformation. Once identifying our passion and cultivating its expression, inspiration fills us and pulls from all of our unique knowing. We are inspired then to express our gifts in totally unique ways.

The importance of the creative spirit transcends the realm of the personal. Only by assuming our rightful roles as creators can we envision new strategies and designs for the continued evolution and survival of the human species. We have witnessed the enormous destructiveness of warfare, ecological disaster, economic chaos, and extreme forms of personal alienation that have plagued the late twentieth and early twenty-first century.

At this critical point in time, our continued social evolution and even survival as a species depends on our harnessing the joint powers of imagination and creativity. Beyond art and invention, these powers must now be applied to the solution of problems in the body politic, in technology, and in systems for human sustenance. The good news is that given these gifts, if we get beyond limited thinking and beliefs we can achieve whatever we truly want for our own good and that of the society as a whole.

People who live as mere consumers are cheating themselves. By acquiescing to a life of mere consumption, people deny themselves the genuine satisfaction that comes from living authentically, expressing their full creative spirit. In the context of a commodified society, creativity has the power to radically transform the self as well as society. By radical, I mean "going to the root or origin; fundamental," that is, it can make a radical difference.

When people are inspired, fear vanishes. Suddenly individuals regain the power to move mountains, so to speak. We have seen how creative people can be when finally they say they've had enough abuse, as in the case of the Occupy movement, which started with just nineteen protestors in New York City. Within a month it had become international, all because people joined together to protest political and financial abuses that had become intolerable and had endured too long.

But when the forces of oppression are not so obvious, and they insidiously grow stronger, we may find ourselves dying by degrees, like the frog being slowly boiled to death… Keeping the creative spirit alive keeps us out of hot water!

Though the original version of this book was written some years ago, I believe the topic of the creative spirit, and the creative process is now more relevant and important than ever. May this book contribute to your own inspiration.

~Karen McChrystal, M.A., March, 2016

Introduction

Creativity has been a little understood process. Most theorists of the creative process, as well as popular understanding, have generally treated it as some mysterious gift possessed only by talented artists or by geniuses. Social scientists who do empirical studies of the creative process have usually chosen as their subjects those who have already distinguished themselves as "creative", and thus, the results of the researches reinforce the notion that creativity is the domain of special people. Artists' recounting of their moments of inspiration continue the mystification: they usually speak of being overcome by some divine or mysterious force which dictates to them, in a state of trance, some message, discovery, new formulation, or artistic inspiration.

Furthermore, most theorists have seen creativity as an effort to compensate for some neurotic fixation from the past, or as merely a way of resolving conflict. Conflict, in this context, is generally seen only in a negative light: it is something bad, dysfunctional. Theorists have not often viewed individual psychic conflict as part of an ongoing dialectical process of the development and growth of the individual. In this light, when psychic conflicts are expressed through some creative medium, creativity may be seen as an expression of health as well as of the neurotic's striving toward healthy resolution of neurotic conflict.

Not until the 1960s humanist self-actualization movement, was creativity thought of as potential in everyone. The humanist psychologists, such as Abraham Maslow, have gone so far as to say, "Even the housewife is creative when she produces an elegant dinner party, complete with her own creations from the kitchen." But few psychologists have begun to understand the dynamics of creativity as a function of human activity in particular.

In discussing creativity as a human activity, we employ a more basic definition of creativity than that which refers only to the production of paintings, novels or musical compositions. For the purposes of the following discussion, I will speak of creativity as being applied imagination. As such, creativity can be seen as being innately human. To quote Karl Marx, "What distinguishes the worst architect from the best of bees is this, that the architect raises his structure in imagination before he erects it in reality." [1] Hence, there is an element of creativity in every deliberate human construction, in the building of cities, in visionary constructs, in the deciphering of ancient languages, in matchmaking, surgery, theses writing – each of these tasks is envisioned in imagination before it is performed.

So, if everyone is doing it, what is the purpose of this book? It would seem, in fact, that fewer and fewer people are capable of sustained creativity, while, paradoxically, an awareness is growing that creativity is innate in everyone. The inhibition of the creative process, furthermore, has dire implications for the psychic health of the individual as well as for the continued evolution of society. (For some psychologists, such as Lawrence Kubie, creativity is nearly synonymous with psychic health). A society that has lost the ability to evolve, that has become rigid, is a society which resorts increasingly to terroristic enforcement of unchanging patterns of behavior, of conformity. The inability to envision a different world is perhaps largely what keeps U.S. policy-makers, for example, locked in to policies which threaten the very survival of the human race – policies dictated by the perceived need to continually increase military spending, even though military spending cannibalizes at a drastic rate the social resources of the global community, so long in the making.

In this book I will attempt to explore and understand current theories of the psychodynamics of the creative process and what blockages to the process occur. The questions then remain of what sparks the imagination, what is the motor force behind the creative effort. From an understanding of individual creativity we must then situate the individual within his society. The inhibitions to creativity have social components, carried over from the past and reinforced daily in the present. Finally, the question remains of how determinant is the social context in its reinforcement of conformist adaptation.

In discussing the shortcomings of current theories of creativity, we turn first to Freud. His model of the creative process is still adequate to explain instances of creative expression: for him, creativity was seen as compensation for thwarted libidinal drives or as the means to resolve libidinal conflicts. The concept of sublimation, that is, the successful channeling of libido into non-sexual activity, does play a part in most creative activity. And Freud presents a coherent, if unelaborated, theory of the ego as being the matrix of creativity – the ego is conceived as the center of awareness of external stimuli, as the storehouse of experiences about them, as that which avoids excessively strong stimuli, adapts to moderate stimuli, and enables activity to bring about changes in the external world. The ego, according to Freud, controls instinctual demands, synthesizes drives, tendencies and functions so that the individual can think, feel and act in an organized, integrated way. From this construct, we can hypothesize a dialectical interaction between the ego and the drives of the libido, or between primary and secondary processes. (Sylvano Arieti is the theorist who more fully articulates this process.) Freud does not, however, conceive of the creative process in the context of the relationship between the individual and society. This limits his analysis to the microcosm of the nuclear family. So Freud must conclude that creativity is, in the final analysis, a compensatory escape from the frustrations and limitations of the nuclear family.

Sylvano Arieti attempts to situate the creative individual within his historical context, recognizing that a particular socio/historical context will contribute to the determination of which individuals actualize their creative potential. But Arieti looks only at the instances of genius, and sees that they are produced during the florescent, developed stages of societies. He does not understand the motivation of the individual to create. While Arieti fully articulates the process of interaction between unconscious, preconscious and conscious components of the psyche in the creative act, he has no notion of desire as the motor of creativity. The limitations of his analysis prevent him from conceiving of social transformation as a creative process. Those who act during periods of social decay in order to create new social arrangements would be invisible to Arieti as creators. Nor does he acknowledge the role of creative individuals in producing what he himself terms the "formative" stage of historical cycles.

Abraham Maslow is less mystified by the creative process. He does recognize a creative potential in everyone. But his analysis of the creative process is purely positivist: he sees the 'self-actualizing individual' developing in a steady progression toward the higher stages of personal development, called 'actualizing', or creative. But within this progression, there is no place for an oppositional relationship to society, a negative view of past experiences, the desire to reject, destroy, or undo any limitations of the social environment. The progression best happens, moreover, when the individual is isolated from the demands of necessity, according to Maslow. The therapeutic technique preferred by Maslow for the encouragement of self-actualization is an 'optimistic attitude' on the part of the therapist, regardless of the conflicts and psychic contradictions affecting the client. The therapist does not engage the client at the level of working through conflict; conflict is, moreover, a little annoyance one must put up with.

Lawrence Kubie has the most fully developed theory of creativity. He does not preclude a notion of conflict, and he does include some understanding of the individual's relation to the outside world. Creativity, for Kubie, is a function of health. Health is based on a balanced relationship between the conscious, the preconscious and the unconscious systems. A rigid anchorage at either end of the system prevents creativity. Kubie also has a minimal concept of the individual's relation to his social context: the preconscious system does not even come into play without the individual's having formulated a conscious choice or goal. The choice or goal actively connects the individual to the external world. Without this, the preconscious process of selection and rejection remains relatively inactive, and the influences which then gain dominance are, according to Kubie, those arising from unconscious fear, guilt, hate, purpose and conflict, or those dependent upon analogic relationships. The fact that Kubie sees these latter influences as being distortions of the creative process sets him apart from most theorists of creativity. The latter include these unconscious motivations within their definition of the creative process. As a result, when they try to locate an ordering principle within the unconscious processes, they do not succeed in finding one. Ehrenzweig, for example, first looks to 'gestalts' as the ordering principle. In his examination of gestalt theories, however, he is able to demonstrate their inadequacies by means of experimentation which indicates that libidinal desire outweighs gestalt principles as an ordering determinant. Ehrenzweig then invents a new construct, the 'undifferentiated matrix,' wherein the ordering process is said to occur, somewhere between the preconscious and the unconscious processes. The libido has a place within this construct, but Ehrenzweig does not elaborate upon its role.

It was the Surrealists, in a cultural movement that began in the early 1920s, who gave primary importance to the role of libidinal drives, which they termed 'desire.' Like Freud, they saw the unconscious as the location of non-contradictory reality, but unlike Freud, they believed the restoration of a non-contradictory, non-fragmented reality could be discovered and extended to the social world, in conjunction with social revolution. They insisted that social revolution was a necessary condition for the liberation of the repressed and the restoration of the balance between the conscious and unconscious forces of the psyche. However, in not understanding the relation between the unconscious and social revolution, finally, they fell back into a non-dialectical view of social relations and art as being separate.

The Situationist International in the 1960's rearticulated the project begun by the Surrealists and took it a step further: they sought to reunite the worlds of the unconscious, art and external reality by attempting to make life itself art. Their emphasis was social – they looked to the 'community of myth' for their artistic unity. But their understanding of psychodynamics was very limited. Hence, they overestimated the independence of the subjective life, the life of desire and imagination, and ended by espousing a type of voluntarism which ignored the strength of the social, and by extension, personal, forces of repression.

A loose synthesis of what is valid in each of these theories might provide a more complete model for the understanding of the creative process. This model must take into account an understanding of the relationship between the conscious and the unconscious forces, the relationship of the external world to the internal world, how the external world reinforces the fragmentation and repression of creative impulses, as well as a notion of practice, or the individual's active refusal of the fragmentation and his assertion of his creative engagement with the social world.

In the following discussion, I will examine these processes and then explore the 'practice' of writing as the activity which can engage the creative processes of the individual and serve to restore a measure of psychological health.

1. Toward an Adequate Theory of Creativity

Theories of creativity have thus far dealt only with fragmentary aspects of the creative process. No one has posited a theory which adequately deals with its totality. Freud defined creativity as the sublimation of sexual frustrations or conflicts; personality theorists attempt to measure experimentally and to categorize traits of those designated 'creative'; current humanist theorists speak of creativity as being the highest stage of development of the human personality and synonymous with peak health; more recent theories attempt to locate the environmental, historical determinants and the psychodynamics of creativity.

As of this writing, no one has tried to account for the dialectic of creativity contained within the continual interaction of the individual with his society. Current theories have a positivist bias which emphasizes the positive resolution of conflict and contradiction and deemphasizes the importance of the negative moment, or those aspects which may be painful, which involve the undoing or destruction of aspects of the past or present in order to make possible something different; furthermore, little attention, if any, is paid to the fostering of creativity as part of the process of social transformation.

FREUD'S MODEL: CONFLICT AND RESOLUTION

The Freudian model remains the most comprehensive, in that it preserves the notion of conflict and resolution. In the notion of sublimation is preserved the idea of conflict: when a sexual desire is in conflict with the demands of reality, the libidinal energy may be desexualized and expressed in another form, i.e., it may be sublimated; resolution of the conflict, the creative moment, is located in the process of sublimation. This is not to say that sublimation is sufficient to produce a work of art. As will later be discussed, discipline and craft is also required. It is, however, in the process of sublimation that eros comes into play in its function of uniting and binding. Eros empowers the ego structure to establish a unity of perception. (In Freud's earlier work, the ego was seen to be an outgrowth of libidinous energy.) According to Freud's early theories, the energy for the work of thought itself must be supplied from sublimated erotic sources.[2]

Before Freud decided that the ego originated from sources other than libido, that the ego had its own 'instincts,' he saw the creative output of the artist as being in inverse proportion to the direct expression of his sexuality. In other words, the less directly sexual expression the artist engaged in, the more libidinal energy he would have left to channel into artistic production. The artistic product was seen as the expression, moreover, of earlier unresolved sexual conflicts, however disguised they reappeared in the artistic product. Freud later rejected the idea of an inverse ratio operating between sexual expression and artistic expression.

In 1920, when Freud again posited a dualism of life and death instincts, he defined eros as the life instinct whose tendency was to reunite, reorganize and form greater and more complex forms of organization. Within this framework, he saw creativity as a function of eros, not necessarily tied to sexual frustration or conflict. The role of the ego remained unclear.

By 1925 the role of the ego was even less clear for the Freudians. Freud compared literary and poetic work to daydreaming and fantasy, as an escape from reality. The realms of daydreaming, fantasy, and art were seen to satisfy the desire for play/pleasure acquired in childhood and never forgotten. Thus, Freud now saw creativity as related more to the pleasure principle, less to the reality principle, and as such, a compensation for unhappiness. He now believed that only unhappy people had daydreams:

> We can begin by saying that happy people never make fantasies, only unsatisfied ones. Unsatisfied wishes are the driving power behind fantasies; every separate fantasy contains the fulfillment of a wish, and improves an unsatisfactory reality.[3]

Freud never wrote about satisfied people who did not fantasize; it would seem that he could only have deduced this conclusion from the confessions of his neurotic patients. He never defines happiness, and claims only to be able to use psychoanalysis to help people have only everyday misery, not neurotic misery. By 1940, Freud was theorizing that the ego derived from a different source than from the libido. As such, the ego was said to have "instincts," which were largely "self-preservative." As mentioned in the Introduction to this book, Freud described the function of the ego, with regard to external events, as the center of awareness of external stimuli, as the storehouse of experiences about them (in the memory), as that which avoids excessively strong stimuli (through flight), deals with moderate stimuli (through adaptation), and brings about expedient changes in the external world (through activity). With regard to internal events, the ego controls instinctual demands. And the ego still has the function of synthesizing drives, tendencies and functions so that the individual can think, feel and act in an organized, integrated way.

From this analysis of psychic structure, creativity might be seen as more autonomous from sexual compensation. In positing the separation of ego and libido, it is possible to assume a more dialectical interaction between the functions of the ego and the drives of the libido, although not until the work of Sylvano Arieti do we see a fully articulated theory of the cooperation between libido and ego, or between primary and secondary processes in the creative process itself. Freud regarded the individual and the nuclear family as representing a microcosm of society at large. Such a vision may preclude the perception of creativity as being a relationship between the individual and society. For Freud, all relationships are reduced to the small circle of the microcosm, wherein the only possible relationships are with other members of the microcosm. Hence, for Freud, creativity was necessarily a compensatory activity – that realm wherein the frustrations and limitations of the nuclear family's psychodynamics could be escaped.

Ivan Pavlov: The "Investigatory" Reflex

It was Ivan Pavlov who in 1927 linked the creative drives of the organism to the outside world by naming the "investigatory" reflex. Such a construct permits the overcoming of the restrictiveness of examining only the relationships within the nuclear family:

> It is this [investigatory] reflex which brings about the immediate response in man and animals to the slightest changes in the world around them, so that they immediately orientate their appropriate receptor organ in accordance with the perceptible quality in the agent bringing about the change, making full investigation of it. The biological significance of this reflex is obvious. If the animal were not provided with such a reflex its life would hang at every moment by a thread. In man this reflex has been greatly developed with far-reaching results, being represented in its highest form by inquisitiveness – the parent of that scientific method through which we hope one day to come to a true orientation in knowledge of the world around us.[4]

Hence, creative adaptation to the environment is an inherent part of the biological nature of man and animal.

SYLVANO ARIETTI: MEN OF GENIUS

Sylvano Arieti takes the frame of reference one step further, once we have escaped the confines of the microcosmic view, by trying to locate creative individuals within their historical epoch. Whereas he shares with Freud the use of the compensation model to explain the motivation for creativity, he also recognizes that a particular socio-historical context will contribute to the determination of which individuals actualize their creative potential.

Arieti documents the occurrence of genius throughout history, pointing out that people of creative genius appear in particularly large numbers during certain periods of history in given geographical areas. He cites the historian Kroeber by way of indicating the relative importance of the influence of environment upon creativity:

> "Inasmuch as even the people possessing higher civilization have produced cultural products of value only intermittently, during relatively small fractions of their time span, it follows that more individuals born with the endowment of genius have been inhibited by the cultural situations into which they were born than have been developed by other cultural situations." [5]

Arieti also cites Charles Edward Gray, who compiled a curve of creativity for Western civilization:

> "Genius emerges in clusters, such blossomings occur several times during a civilization, such peaks are rare and do not characterize most of a civilization's course, and these peaks are of unequal duration." [6]

And, according to Gray's epicycle theory, history is seen as a series of concurrent cycles: an overall economic cycle, a social cycle, and a political cycle. Each of these three cycles goes through four different stages, according to Gray: the formative, the developed, the florescent, and the degenerate. The stages of the four rotate at different speeds. When the florescent and developed stages of the three cycles coincide, we have clusters of creativity. Conversely, when the formative and degenerate stages of different cycles coincide, a falling off of creativity is to be expected. This is the entire scope of historical analysis which Arieti accepts as adequate to his explanation of the occurrence of clusters of creative genius. While this analysis may accurately explain the occurrence of certain types of creativity, that which is nurtured by stability and prosperity, it is not adequate to explain instances of creative activity which occur at any point in a society's development or disintegration.

Arieti's understanding of history and social relations, exemplified for him in the theories of C.E. Gray, then, remains at a level of generality. He does not venture into the area of the relationship of the individual to the structures according to which a society produces itself. In fact, Arieti focuses his attention exclusively on the exceptional individual, the so-called genius, rather than on the average individual, or the averageness of the "genius." For Arieti, it is only the exceptional adolescent who becomes creative:

> The creative adolescent starts to think that his own personal growth will continue if he reaches beyond the limits of what seems to him a restrained and small reality.

He becomes aware of the vast discrepancy between the human condition and the ideals that his cognitive faculties permit him to envision...[7]

Might not this description also apply to the average person, who may or may not have the choice to reach beyond the limits of a restrained reality? The description might also apply to those suffering from paranoid delusions.

Arieti accepts the category "genius" at face value. He does not examine the factors which enable an individual to appear to be a genius, such as freedom from financial worry, support from others who do most of the hard work, as in the case of Leonardo da Vinci, who had a score of young boys to complete each of the projects he began, or early childhood training in the arts, as in the case of Mozart, who received musical instruction from the age of three.

Arieti's only observation about the 'average' person is that very early in life he learns to check his own imagination and to pay more attention to the requirements of reality than to his inner experiences. One might posit more realistically that in most people some combination of idealistic fantasizing, ideal-directed activity, and adjustments to reality or necessity occurs; and, of course, all of the above are subject to environmental factors.

Arieti, like Freud, exhibits a certain fatalism in his understanding of social relations. While he perceives the cyclical nature of the evolution and devolution of societies, he remains ignorant of the specific mechanisms of each social organism, and therefore perceives only epiphenomenonal problems, symptoms of the dynamics of the whole. This brings him full circle back to his pre-occupation with men of genius. To solve the separate problems of hunger, crowding, disease and crime, he recommends that more geniuses make more inventions:

> What is needed is scientific discoveries and inventions to solve the problems originating from increased popu-lation; shortage of food, land, and water; air pollution; decreased supplies of energy; increased rates of certain diseases; crime, and so on... [Also needed are] inno-vations in the fields of ethics, politics, sociology and religion.[8]

Towards the fostering of creativity, Arieti recommends changes in early childhood education. Finally, he makes a half-hearted attempt to describe the qualities of what he calls a "creativogenic society," one which encourages the development of creativity. In so doing, he actually recapitulates the virtues of the liberal bour-geoisie which have been eroded along with the devolution of the entire system. Arieti's list of requisites for a "creativogenic soci-ety" bear a haunting resemblance to the Bill of Rights – what are required are the following:

1. availability of cultural (and certain physical) means ["equal opportunity"];

2. openness to cultural stimuli [commonsense simple psychic health];

3. stress on becoming and not just on being [the pursuit of happiness?];

4. free access to cultural media for all citizens, without discrimination [freedom of the press and of speech?];

5. freedom from discrimination, after severe oppression or absolute exclusion (as with Jews);

6. exposure to different and even contrasting cultural stimuli, tolerance for diverging views, interaction of significant persons [cultural pluralism?];

7. interaction of significant persons, promotion of incentives and awards.

Is this not a blue-print for American liberalism? When Arieti describes what attitudes and conditions would be required for individual fostering of creativity, he again, in microcosm, recapitulates the American liberal leisure-time values: "aloneness, inactivity, daydreaming, free thinking," all of which conditions are presumed to be provided by the system of private domiciles and after-work leisure for every nuclear family unit; and he recommends a "state of readiness for catching similarities, gullibility (i.e., openness, suspension of criticism and judgment), remembrances and inner replaying of past traumatic conflicts (gives form), alertness and discipline." [9] These latter form a good thumbnail sketch of the American liberal white-collar individual, with a little modern psychoanalysis thrown in. What, then, can have prevented there from being more creative activity in the United States?

The attitude of openness and receptivity which Arieti names as prerequisite for creative thinking resembles the surrealist's state of passive receptivity, but he lacks a notion of motivation, namely libidinal drives or desire. He does, however, posit a psychodynamic model which takes a step further Freud's dualistic system of pleasure vs. reality. Arieti proposes a construct, the "tertiary process," to designate a special combination of primary and secondary processes, which synthesis is the location of creativity or innovation. He uses another category, existing within the tertiary process, which accounts for compensatory creativity: synthesis between faulty or archaic and normal mechanisms.10 This latter is the type of creative process with which Freud usually concerned himself.

Arieti calls this synthesis the "magic synthesis." Perhaps his reliance on a notion of magic indicates his lack of understanding of the drive behind creativity – other than that of the idealist special adolescent, or that of neurotic compensation. Arieti's theories are quite adequate in describing how primary process furnishes secondary process with fragments, diffuse, disorganized or primitive material, and how the secondary process shapes the material according to aesthetic or conceptual considerations. But the question of inspiration, for Arieti, is answered by a notion of magic. He does not perceive that the ideals of his 'creative adolescent,' sometimes known as 'desire', may also exist, however suppressed, in most people, and exert a continuous or intermittent pressure, in the form of fantasy, imagination, inspiration, on human consciousness.

ABRAHAM MASLOW AND 'PEAK EXPERIENCE'

The theories of Abraham Maslow suggest, in one sense, an advancement over those of Arieti. Maslow recognizes creativity as potential in everyone. But in failing to understand psychodynamics as outlined by Freud, he misses the mark. He rejects Freud's pleasure/reality duality and instead posits a hierarchy of human psychic development, which moves from "deficiency-needs," such as the needs for food, shelter, security, to "being needs," in which the individual has finally become creative as a "self-actualizer" (SA). Maslow's self-actualizers were described as being:

> ...relatively more spontaneous and expressive than average people, ...more "natural" and less controlled and inhibited in their behavior, which seemed to flow out more easily and freely and with less blocking and self-criticism... SA creativeness was in many respects like the creativeness of all happy and secure children. It was spontaneous, effortless, innocent, easy, a kind of freedom from stereotypes and clichés.[11]

Whereas Maslow has given recognition to the childlike aspects which the modern adult has the luxury to express, largely lacking in the guilt- and reality-bound adults of Freud's time, his construct is still idealistic. For Maslow, to arrive at SA creativity involves no interaction between pleasure and reality; and he ignores the interaction between conflict and resolution and between conscious and unconscious processes. He proposes as therapeutic strategy a type of isolation from reality, a loving cotton-wool insulation:

> The really good therapist who may espouse a pessimistic Freudian theory acts as if growth were possible. The really good teacher who espouses verbally a completely rosy and optimistic picture of human nature, will imply [sic] in actual teaching, a complete understanding and respect for regressive and defensive forces.[12]

In other words, the cure is in the attitude of therapist, who 'respects' all psychic forces, positive and negative, but asserts active understanding of none.

The negative moment thus becomes a mere flaw in the gooey ointment smeared uncritically in the eyes of the individual seeking help in choosing directions for his own development. The non-rosy side of his conflicts are smilingly tolerated as being little annoyances he must put up with. The unconscious is ignored, the negative moments are not worked through, repressed material is less important than "personality". As Russell Jacoby put it in his concise critique of the neo-Freudian "humanist" psychologists,

> Lingering thoughts of neurosis and sickness, doubts about the price and toll of civilized repression, are admitted only to be waved aside as thoughts for and of the sick. A report reaches Allport "that after the turmoil of painful symptoms subsides, many patients still ask the question "what do I live for?" But these distressing cases, however frequent, merely underscore their departure from the human norm.[13]

The premise, in these humanist arguments, is that there is a stage of human development finally to be attained, in which all conflict is transcended, all activity is self-congratulation. From this follows the denial of the negative, the denial of contradiction.

It would seem more accurate to view the self in a constant stage of evolution, of progression from one level of development to the next. As G.F.W. Hegel put it, "this very unrest is the self."[14] To posit an individual free of conflict is mere idealism. Whereas it may be determined whether or not the degree of conflict and the subject's ability to resolve it are neurosis-inducing or not, it is doubtful that there exists a human being free of conflict, or free of a certain tension. Is there not a basic conflict inherent in the dynamic between the build-up of tension (perhaps pleasurable), in the organism and the pleasurable release of tension and return to a state of rest?

Jacoby continues his criticism of the self-styled American existentialists, such as Maslow, accusing them of taking the night out of the day of European existentialism:

> ...within the American scene the negative turns into a positive, an added attraction for the already popular main event. Tragedy, aloneness, death, render life more 'profound'. Maslow talks of the tragic sense of life as if it were the special flavor of the month; it is to spark an otherwise dull selection. It adds a 'dimension of seriousness and profundity of living' which is to be 'contrasted with the shallow and superficial life.' A pinch of death is prescribed as the antidote to the dull life.[15]

In this light, Maslow's 'peak experience,' the high point for his self-actualizers, is the misery of everyday life condensed. Liberation is a banal existence plus enthusiasm. Unable to accept negativity, Maslow is left with the ever-upward progression of the personality toward its lofty peaks of experience which resemble religious ecstasy or Buddhist 'oneness with the world,' where the self is indistinguishable from the world, or does not really exist. All the humanist psychologists have a tendency to think of the integrity of the individual as 'autonomy', isolation from social context. In order to present their 'individual' as separate from society, they must posit the existence of miraculous beings, with special qualities. These so-called humanists ignore the psychodynamics and personal and social history which have produced their 'miraculous beings,' and which are necessary for the development from a level of 'deficiency-needs' to the level of 'being needs.' Maslow writes as one hypnotized by the shining aura of his teachers; he falls into the mode of imitation, much like that of the medieval monk Thomas Kempis, as described in his Imitation of Christ: if one imitates His behavior, surely one will become Christlike. Maslow makes detailed lists of qualities of self-actualizers and of need-cognizants. He divides the world into two groups – the needy neurotics and the successful innocents. With no socio-historical context, no psychodynamics, these types remain fixed in a smiling or frowning universe. His self-actualizers might be sending out beams of uninhibited innocence at the same time as they are fabricating bacteria bombs for military counter-insurgency uses.

The ahistoricity of Maslow's analysis is actually its most grave shortcoming. People who behave creatively in a situation encouraging such, i.e., the warm supportive environment provided by Maslow's uncritical therapists, might, in another situation, be reduced to a level of deficiency-need cognition.

For example, an erstwhile joyful, innocent and creative housewife might, on the occasion of a divorce, no longer be able to afford a therapist, and might, in fact, have to find work. Having no job skills, she might find herself taking work in a factory. The other women in the factory, never having had the privileges once enjoyed by our housewife, might regard her with jealousy, resentment and hostility. This formerly self-actualizing woman, might, in this situation for which she possessed no social skills, very well regress to a state of deficiency-need cognition: she would probably feel insecure, without a sense of belongingness, identification, respect or prestige, all listed by Maslow as needs at the deficiency level.

Contrariwise, a child raised in a highly neurotic nuclear family, in which the parents were incapable of giving love, might blossom overnight in the company of, say, a teacher giving special classes, who was clearly trustworthy, caring for the child, giving of respect, fairness, consistency.

The qualities Maslow enumerates as those possessed by self-actualizing creative people then, may be seen as potentially present in anyone, depending on several factors: psycho-social history, current practice, historical circumstances, and attendant present and future expectations. The question for theorists of creativity now remains as 'how to get there.'

Maslow contributes some insight into depth psychology in his modification of Freud's understanding of primary process. Freud sees the latter as "dangerous" forbidden id impulses, deeply repressed. Maslow saw primary process as composed not of repressed material, but as "forgotten" or suppressed material, put aside because of the purposeful and pragmatic demands of a harsh reality.

LAWRENCE KUBIE AND THE ROLE OF CONSCIOUS CHOICE OR GOAL-SETTING

Lawrence Kubie[16] has a more psychodynamic understanding of creative processes. Like Maslow, he sees creativity as a function of health, but unlike Maslow and the existential humanist psychologists, he avoids the superficiality which results from belittling the importance of the negative moment. In going back to Freud's more precise categorization of non-conscious processes, Kubie is able to distinguish between the more deeply buried (accessible only through translation) levels of pain and conflict, and the intuitive and learned patterns of behavior which are capable of becoming conscious with varying degrees of effort. The former is the 'unconscious' system; the latter, the 'preconscious'. When there are deep level conflicts or pain within an individual's unconscious, they must be purged. But when the psyche is freed from these preoccupations, the individual may maintain the alliance between the preconscious and the conscious system, which alliance, for Kubie, equals health and permits creativity.

The preconscious, in addition to retaining learned patterns of behavior, such as walking, talking, playing music, is where allegorical and figurative uses of symbolic processes occur. The preconscious possesses less mature symbolic functions than the conscious, retaining a broad overlapping base of multiple meanings, by which the enormous creative leaps of intuitive functions may be made. The contribution of the PCS (preconscious system) processes to creativity depends upon their freedom in gathering, assembling, comparing and reshuffling of ideas. The rigid anchorage at either the UCS (unconscious system) or the CS (conscious system) end of the psychic system prevents this fluidity.

Kubie understands the conscious process to include an aspect of praxis, a relation to the 'real' world. The preconscious system does not come into play without a conscious choice or goal being formulated:

> The choice of any topic for discussion sets in motion automatic preconscious processes of selection and rejection from among all possible elements in stream of association. Contrariwise, whenever we allow our thoughts to roam without a preselected goal, the process of automatic preconscious selecting and rejecting re¬mains relatively inactive, exposing (a) the influences arising from unconscious fear, guilt, hate, purpose, and conflict; (b) those influences which are dependent upon analogic relationships in the associative stream (from which all creativity derives); and (c) those which emanate from concurrent physiological variables.[17]

Arieti, without a concept of choice in his theory, understands the laws of association only in terms of analogic or proximate associations. For Kubie, on the other hand, choice, or goal, is a requisite to health (psychic). According to him, absence of conscious choice results in passivity of preconscious processes, thereby giving inordinate influence to the unconscious. If the unconscious is dominant in such a manner, the result is illness, says Kubie.

The notion of conscious choice does not preclude the process of free association. In fact, for Kubie, free association is the natural process by which man creates, the essential instrument in the process of the creative search.[18] The preliminary goal or choice is that which anchors the preconscious to some point in 'reality' and initiates the process of free association.

ANTON EHRENZWEIG: "THE HIDDEN ORDER OF ART"

There seems to be a contradiction within this construct, however. Not until the Surrealists' experimentation with automatism was the contradiction revealed: Surrealists poets could begin merely to write whatever came to mind, claiming to have no preconceptions, no preliminary goals or choices. Perhaps the choice to write, rather than just to think, was the necessary catalyst.

Anton Ehrenzweig, in his study of the psychology of artistic imagination, looked for an order within the unconscious to explain "the hidden order of art." He found inadequate Otto Rank's attempts to explain art by pointing out the elements of primary process. For Ehrenzweig the occasional intrusions of dream material into art...

...did not add up to an exhaustive catalogue of all possible art forms, even if one excluded the deliberately
composed patterns of art's (conscious) superstructure...
It was impossible to describe the spontaneously created
components of art, such as textures, in terms of dream
techniques. They often lack any structure that could be
analyzed in terms of definite patterns. These spontaneous (unconsciously controlled) elements – artistic handwriting and textures both in the visual arts and in music
– have none of the rigor and good gestalt that character-
ize the conscious superstructure of art. Owing to their
apparent lack of organization they cannot be identified as
condensations, displacements and the like, as the forms
of a joke can; rather they demonstrate the chaos and dis-
organization which psychoanalytic ego psychology is all
ready to associate with unconsciously produced forms.[19]

Gestalt psychology, then, was also inadequate for Ehrenzweig, for
it posits a level of order too highly developed, too clearly defined,
characteristic of the conscious superstructure of art more than
of the unconscious roots of creation. And whereas the gestaltists
posit that there is a gestalt ordering present in human beings
from birth, Ehrenzweig cited studies refuting this. Children born
blind, for example, who later gained sight, were observed to have
a libidinous interest in reality which outweighed gestalt perception as their greatest and most efficient guide. The gestalt theory
hypothesized that these newly-sighted people would at once
focus their attention upon simple basic geometric patterns, like
spheres and circles, cubes and squares, pyramids and triangles,
those shapes which constituted 'good' gestalt patterns standing out

from a blurred ground. These patients, in fact encountered incredible difficulties when suddenly faced with the complexities of the visual world. Many of them could not muster the effort needed for organizing the buzzing chaos of colored blotches. Some of them felt profound relief when blindness overcame them once again and allowed them to sink back into their familiar world of touch. On the other hand, a girl who was an animal lover identified her beloved dog first of all. A recent case showed that the face of the physician was the first shapeless blob picked out from the general blur of the visual field.[21] Ehrenzweig cites another case where a young baby will smile at a terrifying crude mask if only it has certain minimum cues suggesting the mother's face, but will show signs of fear if the cues are missing.

Hence, Ehrenzweig concludes that there is no innate gestalt perception, but rather a unity of understanding, even in childhood perception, an undifferentiated or 'syncretistic' vision, which is fragmented during adolescence into the conceptual and the intuitive functions, no longer one.

Ehrenzweig formulated the construct of an "undifferentiated matrix," located beneath the more superficial, although gestalt-ordered, condensations, displacements and other so-called primary process forms. The latter are secondary, imposed upon the "truly unconscious" undifferentiated matrix, similar to the child's primitive vision of the world. Theories of perception are used to describe the interaction between id fantasies and this structure:

Perception sets apart from the outset a large part – perhaps even much the larger part – of its function as an unconscious subliminal substructure into which id fantasy can penetrate with the greatest ease. The ease of the id's penetration is, of course, explained by the extreme undifferentiation of unconscious vision. Its wide all-embracing sweep can use almost any object form as an assembly point for an immense cluster of other images that, for conscious analytic vision at least, have nothing in common.[22]

Ehrenzweig's concept is much less rigid than those previously discussed in this chapter. Unlike gestalt configurations, the undifferentiated matrix is fluid, newly formed for each set of perceptions.

Ehrenzweig's recognition of libido as the directional motivation which structures perception gives him a more comprehensive perspective than have the gestaltists, who posit an "élan toward gestalt completion," and a broader perspective than that of Kubie, who posits "goal" or "choice" as necessary. The libidinal motivation theory could explain the automatism of the Surrealists.

THE SURREALISTS: ORDER WITHIN THE UNCONSCIOUS

The Surrealists also believed there to be an order within the unconscious (loosely defined), and wished to resolve the dichotomy between dream and reality to create a kind of absolute reality, a surreality. They understood Freud to posit the unconscious as the location of a noncontradictory reality, free from repression, temporality, and composed of psychic realities obedient to the pleasure principle and to no other. Through the method of automatism (automatic painting or writing), they believed themselves to be reaching directly into the unconscious. They did not distinguish among various levels of the unconscious, however; they posited dreams as being the repository of the unconscious order. As their main purpose was the restoration of a liberatory unity to the entire social order, the *sine qua non* of which was the social revolution, they were not very concerned with making a more detailed analysis of the structure of the unconscious. They did derive a classification system for imagery produced by automatic writing, which contains psychoanalytic as well as literary criteria, and remains unrigorous:

> ...their [surrealist images'] greatest virtue is the one that is arbitrary to the highest degree, the one that takes the longest time to translate into practical language, either because it contains an immense amount of seeming contradiction or because one of the terms is strangely concealed; or because, presenting itself as something sensational, it seems to end weakly (because it suddenly closes the angle of its compass), or because it derives from itself a ridiculous formal justification, or because it is of an hallucinatory kind, or because it very naturally gives to the abstract the mask of the concrete, or the opposite, or because it implies the negation of some elementary physical property, or because it provokes laughter.[23]

The importance of the Surrealists' attempts lies in their having illustrated in their poetry, prose, painting, dancing, the evidence, the products, of the continuous voice of the unconscious (or pre-conscious), and in having insisted upon the necessity of social revolution as a condition for the liberation of the repressed and the restoration of the balance between the conscious and unconscious forces of the psyche. What they neglected to do was to clarify the relation between the expressions of the unconscious and social revolution. Consequently, they fell back into a dichotomous view and designated 'art' as the realm of the unconscious and separate from social relations.

Finally, the surrealist attempt was cut short with the defeat of the revolutionary pulse around the world. Stalinism, World War II, and what might have been seen as the success of capitalism's post-war consolidation discouraged the further development of surreal-ist theory and practice for the time being.

THE SITUATIONIST INTERNATIONAL

In the 1960's, the Situationist International, in Europe, rearticu-lated the project begun by the Surrealists, but in a more integrated manner: they no longer accepted art as a realm separate from 'reality', but sought to make life itself a work of art (as discussed in Chapter 2). They looked not to the deep order of the psyche for unity, but to the community which could be created with the supersession of the society based on myth:

> By losing the community of the society of myth, society must lose all the references of a really common language, up to the moment when the separation of the inactive

community can be surmounted by accession to the real historical community. Art was the common language of social inaction; from the moment when it constitutes itself into independent art in the modern sense, emerging from its original religious universe and becoming individual production of separate works, it knows, as a special case, the movement which dominates the history of the ensemble of separate culture. Its independent affirmation is the beginning of its destruction.[24]

While the S.I. had little articulated understanding of psychodynamics, they intuitively grasped that "desire" was the motor force necessary to counteract the accumulated repressions of history, specifically, of capitalism. For them the concept of desire encompassed more than Ehrenzweig's concept of libido, which he mentions almost in passing. Desire was for the Situationists more akin to 'eros,' as Freud used the term to designate 'life instinct.' Desire includes imagination as well as reason which partakes of the sensibilities of the pleasure principle as well as of the reality principle. In their wish to counteract the rigidities of late capitalism, however, the S.I. overemphasized the role of the subjective life, thereby underestimating the strength of the repressive forces still active within the capitalist mode. Their conclusions were only partially correct: they analyzed the failings of the current system in terms of the boredom (read 'stasis') of everyday life and ignored the economic efficiencies introduced by the capitalist mode:

Capitalist production has unified space, which is no longer bounded by external societies. This unification is at the same time an extensive and intensive process of banalization. The accumulation of commodities produced on the assembly line for the abstract space of the market, which broke through all regional and legal barriers and all the corporate restrictions of the middle ages that preserved the quality of craft production, also destroyed the autonomy and quality of places. This power of homogenization is the heavy artillery which brought about the fall of all the walls of China.[25]

And,

A new form of mental illness has swept the planet: banalization. Everyone is hypnotized by work and by comfort: by the garbage disposal unit, by the elevator, by the bathroom, by the washing machine.[26]

The lasting contribution of the Situationists was their articulation of the possibilities for a world in which the individual and his/her environment would be suited to a continuously creative alliance of 'pleasure' and 'reality' principles, of psyche and material reality: in their theory for 'revolutionary urbanism,' they delineated uses of technology which "could allow an unbroken contact between the individual and cosmic reality – minus some of whatever one considers its asperities."[27] Basic to their new civilization would be the construction of situations. This need for total creation has always been inseparable from the need to play with architecture: to play with time and space.

...Architecture is the simplest way of articulating time and space; of modulating reality; of making people dream...

...This new vision of time and space, which will be the theoretical basis of future constructions, is still imprecise and will remain so until there has been real practical experimentation with possible patterns of behavior in towns designed solely to this end: towns which, apart from the few buildings strictly necessary for some degree of comfort and security, would consist solely of buildings highly charged with emotionally evocative power, buildings one can feel, symbolical buildings representing desires, powers, events from the past, the present and future. A rational extension of traditional religious experience, of myths, of fairy-tales and, above all, of psychoanalysis into architectural expression becomes more and more urgent every day...as every reason for falling in love disappears.[28]

The optimism and vision of the Situationists was fueled by the revolutionary turbulence of the prosperity and increased expectations of the late 1950's and the 1960's. They had only time to begin to articulate a vision before the armed might of the State and the beginnings of the economic downturn took the wind out of their sails. The task of fueling the flame of revolutionary creativity and vision in the present period of apparent scarcities of everything vital to continued human life (including reason) is no easy one. In every epoch, however, a few individuals remain undaunted and keep alive their creativity. It will be the attempt of the following discussions to elucidate how this is possible, to understand what prevents creativity in particular individuals, and outline broad approaches for getting touch with creative powers.

2. Freedom and the Imagination

In speaking of creativity, we are speaking of the use of the faculty of imagination, the ability to envision that which is not yet apparent or not yet present in reality. We might call imagination the stimulating principle of the mind. It is that which unifies the various aspects of sensible intuition.[29] It is through imagination that one may envision alternatives to any given reality, and thus envision the possibilities for freedom from the strictures or determinations of one's condition.

For Edgar Allen Poe, imagination is the queen of the faculties. He does not mean fantasy or sensibility. For Poe, rather, according to Charles Baudelaire,

> ...the imagination is a faculty that is almost divine and that perceives from the very first moment, by ways other than those of the philosopher, the intimate and secret relations between things, their correspondences and analogies.[30]

If we see imagination as that by which intuition is brought into mental focus, synthesized, given meaning, and that by which alternate realities are envisioned, then the loss of imagination implies the loss of human freedom. Psychology and psychoanalysts have generally envisioned freedom as freedom from neurosis rather than as freedom to create something new. According to Sigmund Freud *(The Ego and the Id)*, the imagination is necessary to the preservation of health insofar as it is necessary to the successful sublimation of drives and impulses. According to Freud *(Civilization and its Discontents)*, Western civilization demands the suppression of instinct, which creates conflict and frustration for the individual which results in neuroses. The only alternative to neurosis is to channel these drives into less direct modes of expression, such as art, invention or religion, which can be acceptable to society.

It is, of course, possible to point to artists, poets, musicians and painters who in their personal lives have exhibited marked manifestations of psychological disturbance. However, it would probably be best to say that their creative lives were fruitful and productive in spite of, rather than because of, such psychological difficulties.

So with the psychoanalysts, Freud in particular, we have at base a functional view of the imagination: it is necessary to prevent neurosis, and produces interesting works of art. The imagination was not viewed so much in its own right, as the motor of creativity, and was not considered in the light of being essential to social evolution except in a limited way: Freud did not envision the possibility of a higher stage of social evolution except that brought about by helping people, through psychoanalysis, to have to live with only everyday misery rather than with neurotic misery.

THE NECESSITY FOR ENVISIONING
A DIFFERENT WORLD

From the vantage point of the present, it is perhaps easier to envision a different social order, even if only because we have witnessed the enormous destructiveness of warfare, ecological disaster, economic chaos, and extreme forms of personal alienation that have plagued the late twentieth century. The envisioning of a different possible world is also made easier by the fact that now there is available the technological and material means for the reordering and redistribution of the means of the production of social wealth. Imagination and creativity are vital if humanity is to survive at all, and imagination must be turned to the creation of social vision. No longer is the role of imagination limited to art, invention, or religion, but there is now the possibility of applying imagination to the solution of problems in the realms of technology, the organization of society and its own reproduction.

Some writers have glimpsed some of the profound implications of the use of imagination as important to the fulfillment of human destiny. Henry Miller is one such:

> From the beginning almost I was deeply aware that there is no goal. I never hope to embrace the whole, but merely to give in each separate fragment, each work, the feeling of the whole as I go on, because I am digging deeper and deeper into life, digging deeper and deeper into past and future. With the endless burrowing a certitude develops which is greater than faith or belief. I become more and more indifferent to my fate, as writer, and more and more certain of my destiny as man.[31]

And Katherine Ann Porter:

> Any true work of art has got to give you the feeling of
> reconciliation – what the Greeks would call catharsis,
> the purification of your mind and imagination – through
> an ending that is endurable because it is right and true.[32]

In fact, in modernist art itself is implicit the use of imagination for
the creation of social vision. As Thomas Wolfe put it,

> It is not merely that in the cultures of Europe and of the
> Orient the American artist can find no antecedent scheme,
> no structural plan, no body of tradition that can give his
> own work the validity and truth that it must have. It is
> not merely that he must make somehow a new tradition
> for himself, derived from his own life and from the enor-
> mous space and energy of American life, the structure of
> his own design; it is not merely that he is confronted by
> these problems; it is even more than this – that the labor
> of a complete and whole articulation, the discovery of
> an entire universe and of a complete language is the task
> that lies before him.[33]

The creative process, then, is that through which man expresses
his unique nature as a radiating center of meaning and as a future
creating being. By the term 'meaning,' here, I mean a unified set
of perceptions, which, for the individual, is shaped according to
his needs and desires in the context of his relationship with the
world. The envisioning of a future will include the perspective of
the individual's needs and desires, as well as his understanding of
the realm of the possible.

And creativity is ultimately a social process. An individual does not create within a vacuum peopled only by his own existence. Every human creation partakes of ideas and information emanating from the social world, and from the surrounding environment. As experimentally demonstrated by Jose Delgado after a detailed study of neuron pathways and the synapses which permit new connections between circuits,

> "The brain can accept, reject or react against received information, or establish associations between past and present sensory inputs. Originality and invention are merely a novel combination of old data, and original thought could not be produced by the naive brain of a newborn baby."[34]

Whereas the ancients thought inspiration was a gift from the gods, we may now understand it to emanate from a particular relationship with the world. When an individual focuses his attention on a particular problem or aspect of his world and brings the various aspects of his own psyche into resonance with this external focus, a new unity of perception or understanding nay arise between the internal and external aspects, as resolution or inspiration. Further on this will be discussed in greater detail.

THE DOMINATION OF SUBJECTIVE LIFE, OR, WHAT INHIBITS CREATIVITY?

What is this increasingly powerful organization of the world of things and systems of frozen roles and social relationships, and why does it seem able increasingly to dominate the subjective world, the world of human desires, consciousness and imagination? It is the order of the marketplace, which changes all qualities into quantities and judges their worth according to yet another quantity – the price thereto affixed. Likewise, human beings are judged only according to the contribution they make to the accumulation of global capital.*

Note: "Capital," as minimally defined by Marx, is accumulated labor power, or the congealed historic relationships between those who own the means of production and those who sell their labor to them. More concretely, capital can take many forms: stock certificates, fixed plant, inventories of commodities awaiting sale, and so on. But the heart of the congealed relationships is productive wage labor: wage workers are productive in the capitalist sense when they produce in their day's work a value of commodities which is greater than the value of their day's wages. This greater value, surplus value, is realized as profit through the sale of the commodities and reinvested as new raw materials, fixed plant, and workers. But capital exists only as many capitals – fixed, circulating, and constant – e.g., firms, industries, whole national economies. Each capital is driven to maximize surplus value, to grow, by the pressure of competition from others. Capital as a whole is thus inherently expansionist. It tends to dominate more and more of the world and convert more and more people into wage workers and commodity consumers. Through the commodities its workers produce, capital penetrates all aspects of social life and transforms them according to its own blind, flatly quantitative needs.

What circulates through this global organization of the world of quantities, the objective world, is not predominantly human creativity, but rather the exchange of commodities. Social relations are subordinated to and concealed by the latter.

As Georg Lukacs explains,

> In this situation a man's own activity, his own labor, becomes something objective and independent of him, something that controls him by virtue of an autonomy alien to man.[35]

The world of objects and relations between things spring into a kind of life of their own, within the movement of commodities through the market system. Even when economists gradually discover the laws governing these objects, they still appear to have an invisible force, generating their own power. An individual aware of these laws is still unable to modify the process by his own activity. His activity itself becomes estranged from him as it is turned into a commodity which is also subject to the non-human laws of the marketplace.

Not only is the worker separated from any meaningful relationship to the product of his labor, his labor itself has become increasingly fragmented through the Taylorization* of white-collar as well as of blue-collar jobs. Work is reduced to the mechanical repetition of increasingly specialized sets of actions; the worker becomes the "mass worker," indifferent to the particular content of the job, because it is all equally meaningless, except for the price paid for the work and the pleasantness, however shallow, of the company of co-workers.

Note: By "taylorization," we mean the breaking down of complex, multiple job operations which require a variety of skills into the simplest possible components, each carried out by a single worker, such that skill, and thus control of the work process, is effectively taken out of the hands of the worker and concentrated in the hands of management. For an account of this process, see Braverman, Harry, *Labor and Monopoly Capital,* especially Chapter 4, "Scientific Management." [36]

The fragmentation of the process of production necessarily entails the fragmentation of its subject. In consequence of the technical rationalization of the work-process, the human qualities and idiosyncrasies of the worker appear increasingly as mere sources of error when contrasted with these abstract special laws functioning according to rational predictions. Man is no longer the authentic master of the process; on the contrary, he is a mechanical part incorporated into a mechanical system.[35] Denied any active role for his intelligence, apart from creative adaptation, rebellion, or organized opposition, his creative powers of cognition are largely suppressed, as is his will. He is forced into an increasingly contemplative or neurotic position. And to assert an individual distinction of character or to suggest that the inner self is constantly changing, is to experience a threat to ones identity as part of the outer world and its laws of the market.

* * *

With the fragmentation of the human subject comes the loss of the ability to conceive of the world as a meaningful, organized whole. Gestalt psychology has shown there to be a direct relationship between the ability to conceive of meaningful totalities (or gestalts) and neurosis and psychosis. In health, according to Gestalt theory, there is a flexible interplay of figure formation (the perceptual focus upon an object or figure) with its background. Healthy figure-ground formation is characterized by "attention, concentration, interest, concern, excitement and grace," according to Frederick ("Fritz") Perls, daddy of gestalt therapy.[38] With the disturbance of healthy figure-ground formation comes confusion, boredom, compulsions, fixations, anxiety, amnesias, stagnation, and self-consciousness (in the sense of awkwardness).

These dysfunctions may be seen to be induced, at least in part, by the process of work and survival in the modern world. Boredom results from meaninglessness experienced by the mass worker. Stagnation of the mental faculties is nearly always the result of boredom. There is no question that anxiety is difficult for most people to avoid, subject as they are to constant stress. With the general dulling of the senses through boredom and stagnation, the erosion of the senses through anxiety, comes the breakdown of gestalt formation, resulting in the formation of neurotic symptoms, as mentioned above.

With regard to amnesia, it is, at a certain level, broadly induced by the dictates of the economic system. As Russell Jacoby put it,

The intensification of the drive for surplus value (profit) accelerates the rate at which past goods are liquidated to make way for new goods; planned obsolescence is everywhere, from consumer goods to thinking to sexuality. Built-in obsolescence exempts neither thought nor humans. What is heralded as new or young in things, thoughts, or people masks the constant: this society.[39]

So the question remains as to how it is conceivable that one, whose character is determined by capitalist culture, could free himself of the determinations of alienated social relations. How can an individual within capitalist society base his identity on a non-capitalist set of identity criteria and world outlook and acquire knowledge outside the bounds of capitalist epistemology?[40]

While the home once provided the comforting and replenishing retreat, the separations between the world of work and the world of leisure have increased. The private sphere is eroded at once by shrinking purchasing power and by the organization of leisure by the leisure industry, in particular, the media. Max Horkheimer describes the process:

The gradual dissolution of the family, the transformation of personal life into leisure and of leisure into routines supervised to the last detail, into the pleasures of the ball park and the movie, the best seller and the radio, has brought about the disappearance of the inner life.[41]

Before high culture was replaced by these manipulated pleasures, passively consumed, one could flee into a private conceptual world and rearrange thoughts to then rearrange reality. With the loss, or rather, the surrendering of this refuge, there is no longer an easily available realm for the conceptualizing of a world different from the given.

THE RESTORATION OF SUBJECTIVITY AND THE LIBERATION OF THE SUBJECT

Within the society dominated by the organization of objective life, that is, the society of the spectacle, where nearly every human activity and its products are sold into the service of the dominant culture, and when no dialogue is permitted between the individual and his creations, the individual must appear as a contemplative or frenetic being, at best, and as an automaton, neurotic, or psychotic at worst. In the contemplative, psychic life rages unseen beneath the calm surface; in the frenetic, life simply rages, uncontrolled (witness the 'impulsive character' or the psychopath). In both cases, the ego and id, instinctual energies and directions, rationality and imagination "are withdrawn from the repressive socialization and strive toward autonomy, albeit in a 'fictitious world' of fantasy," according to Marcuse,[42] or through violent destruction of the social order.

Within the withdrawal into the 'fictitious' world, however, is the possibility for a creative approach: the restructuring of consciousness (which is not to deny or ignore the transformative powers of violence).

By 'fictitious' is meant the relationship to reality, not the absence of reality. All conscious contents of the mind – perception,

imagery, memory, thinking, feeling, and imagination – are pow-
ered by a fusion of outer and inner drives. The stimuli from the
real world of moving people and relationships must be integrated
with stimuli from the inner flux of remembered imagery, motor
tendencies, and unconsciously produced metaphor, images, symbols, and concepts. It is when the inner drives are withdrawn from
the lockstep relation to alienated routine, the immediate world
of survival and labor, that the energies may be turned to different perspectives, to creative imagination. The latter perspective
is 'fictitious' in that it occurs at a remove from the immediate,
but it does not exclude perceptions of reality. It may include a
comprehension of the totality, or different relationships among the
parts, among the inner contents of the mind, the flux of remembered imagery, metaphor, images, concepts. The new relationships
may be formed more in accordance with inner needs and desires
than in accordance with external dictates. For a healthy restructuring of consciousness the stimuli from the real world must be
integrated with the stimuli from the inner drives, but the balance
will be shifted, the relationships freed enough from the reality
principle to enable this restructuring. If reality is ignored and the
unconscious should become dominant, there will occur an explo-
sion of neurosis or psychosis. When the ego, the filter for perceiving and structuring 'reality,' and the unconscious fail to communicate, through sublimation or through acting to obtain immediate
gratification, the neurotic imbalance will again result. This will
take the form of rigidity, stereotypy: the storing in the unconscious

of fragments of experience that were stopped in their development. According to gestalt psychology, each of the incompleted patterns contains its own tendency, or élan, toward completion. It is this élan which psychotherapy presumably attempts to promote as well as to remove blockages to this process of self-completion.

The inherent élan is the power which propels the evolution of the species, be it through creative imagination, sublimation, or through social transformation. The reconciliation of all fragmented parts of the psyche has been held by some to be a revolutionary necessity. Most prominent among these were the Surrealists, a group of radical artists and writers who came together first in Europe in the early 1900's. Their efforts were directed toward the following:

> ...to set up a line of communication between the over-dissassociated worlds of sleep and wakefulness, of interior and exterior reality, of reason and folly, of the calm of knowledge and of love, of life and of Revolution.

> ...These antinomies, cruelly felt, must be gotten rid of, implying as they do a servitude deeper, more definitive than any other, must not find man resigned.[43]

The Surrealists believed there was a point, which they called "the supreme point," from which all contradictions would be no longer perceived as antinomies:

> Everything leads us to believe that there is a certain point in the spirit from which life and death, real and

imaginary, past and future, communicable and incommunicable are no longer perceived as contradictories. It would be vain to look for any other motivation in surrealist activity than the hope of determining this point.[44]

The Surrealists' technique for getting to this point was to use trance, wandering, or automatic writing, which they thought was the direct route to the unconscious. With this technique, they did indeed write poetry and prose containing relationships never before expressed, and often achieved a rare beauty, as in this poem by Benjamin Peret:

LOBSTER

The egrets of your voice springing from the
burning bush of your lips
in which the Chevalier de la Barre would be
happy to be consumed
the sparrow-hawks of your eyes catching
without realizing it
all the sardines in my head
your breath of wild pansies
reflecting from the ceiling on my feet
go through and through me
follow me or go before
send me to sleep and wake me
throw me out of the window to make me
come up by lift, and vice versa

The efforts of the Surrealists could only indicate directions for the liberation of the human spirit, for conditions, objective and subjective, were not yet ripe. Some became communists, having realized the continuing necessity to transform the world at the level, of objective reality. The prevailing economic system daily recreated the fine web of reification. On the question of liberation, they said:

> In reality we are faced with two problems, one of which is the problem raised, at the beginning of the twentieth century, by the discovery of the relations between the conscious and the unconscious. That was how the problem chose to present itself to us... We hold the liberation of man to be the sine qua non of the liberation of the mind, and we can expect this liberation of man to result only from the proletarian revolution.[45]

Marcuse's position on art comes close to that of the Surrealists. He envisioned the function of art as a process of envisioning liberation as well as of asserting it: the process of art is the movement of subjectivity, restructuring the relationships among and between desire and reality; the artistic product contains the vision of the new reality:

> Art explodes the given reality in the name of a truth normally denied or even unheard. The inner logic of the work of art terminates in the emergence of another reason, another sensibility, which defy the rationality and sensibility incorporated in the dominant social institutions... The transcendence of immediate reality shatters the reified objectivity of established social relations and

opens a new dimension of experience: rebirth of rebellious subjectivity.[46]

Great art is interdependent with the times it reflects and transcends. The direction of evolution of the society will determine in part the degree to which imagination will be able to contribute to the social evolution, and the uses to which it is put. Henri Miller presents an optimistic view of the future of the imagination as embodied in art, and the imagination of the future:

> Art is only a means to life, to the life more abundant. It is not in itself the life more abundant. It merely points the way... All art, I firmly believe, will one day disappear. But the artist will remain and life itself will become not "an art," but art... In any true sense we are certainly not yet alive. We are no longer animals, but we are certainly not yet men. ...Once art is really accepted it will cease to be. It is only a substitute, a symbol language, for something which can be seized directly. But for this to become possible man must become thoroughly religious, not a believer, but a prime mover, a god in fact and deed. He will become that inevitably. And of all the detours along this path, art is the most glorious, the most fecund, the most instructive. The artist who becomes thoroughly aware consequently ceases to be one. And the trend is towards awareness, towards that blinding consciousness in which no present form of life can possibly flourish, not even art.[47]

The Situationist International, a group of theorists and political activists writing in Paris in the late nineteen sixties, pronounced the death of art and strove to merge art and life immediately. They criticized as inadequate the assaults made by the Surrealists and the Dadaists, whom they took to be historically related and opposed. Each movement had developed a one-sided critique:

> Dadaism wanted to suppress art without realizing it; surrealism wanted to realize art without suppressing it. The critical position later elaborated by the Situationists has shown that the suppression and the realization of art are inseparable aspects of the overcoming of art.[48]

The central thesis of the Situationists was that art, in all its traditional forms, was completely played out. The end of western culture had been marked by the Dadaist movement; no major self-regeneration was possible. But at the same time, western civilization had reached the point where mechanization and automation had, potentially, eliminated the need for almost all traditional forms of labor, opening up perspectives of unprecedented leisure. The Situationists, using the ideas of the Surrealist, Tristan Tzara, suggested that,

> ...this leisure could only be filled by a new type of creativity – a creativity that started where 'art' left off. Imagination should be applied directly to the transformation of reality itself, not to its symbols in the form of philosophy, literature, painting, etc. Equally, this transformation should not be in the hands of a small body of specialists but should be made by everyone. It was normal everyday life that should be made passionate and rational and dramatic, not its reflection in a separated

'world of art.' The modern artist does not paint but creates directly... Life and art make One.[49]

And the point was not just the creation of an exterior environment, however vast or however lovely. What they felt necessary was that everyone discover within himself desires for particular environments in order to make them real. This attitude was diametrically opposed to that of the neo-Freudian groups, who advocate, moreover, the reconciliation between desire and reality. The Situationists insisted that "everyone must search for what they love, for what attracts them..." [50] The point was the conjuring up and the mastery of immediate subjective experience. "Art need no longer be an account of past sensations. It can become the direct organization of more highly evolved sensations. It is a question of producing ourselves, not things that enslave us." [51] The situationist project, as originally outlined, was the liberation of desire in the building of a new world – "a world with which we will be permanently in love." [52]

The social upheaval of 1968 which gave inspiration and energy to this vision subsided under the weight of the whole old world. Routine, repression and 'reality', or necessity, sealed over the fissures in the old order, from which had emerged this glimpse of a new world.

Having glimpsed the possibilities for a world which nurtures and is nurtured by creative inspiration, we must ask how the creative process may be sustained between periods of social upheaval. How is it that the individual imagination may escape burial by routine and repression, by necessity? The realm of necessity is diminished or modified by human creativity. It is true during any period that everyone must search for what they love, for what attracts them. The single sparks of creativity gradually become more frequent again, and dissolve into a single light, the promise of a new upsurgence of the powers of social transformation. In the following chapter I will recount the experiences of several writers in their moments of creative inspiration. A discussion of the psychodynamics of creativity, as potentially manifest in everyone, will follow.

3. The Creative Process: Manifest and Latent

C hroniclers of the creative, or artistic process, as well as creators and artists themselves, have often been mystified as to the source of inspiration. Some consider it akin to the ineffable. Stanwood Cobb, a psychologist, says,

> A strange cosmic energy seems to take possession of man as creator, to endow him with something of vision and of creative power which is more universal than the scope of his own personality or human experience.[53]

Ralph Waldo Emerson called it the "oversoul"; Brahms sees it as a cosmic force:

> Then when I felt those cosmic vibrations, I knew that I was in touch with the same Power that inspired those great poets, and also Bach, Mozart and Beethoven. Then the ideas that I was consciously seeking flowed in upon me with such force and speed that I could only grasp and hold a few of them...[54]

The creative process manifest with writers and poets will be explored in this chapter (which is not to discount the creativity involved in the sudden surge of insight, the 'gift' of inspiration, which occurs for scientists, mathematicians, detectives, and others involved in inventing something new under the sun).

The accounts of literary inspiration are numerous. Most involve an idea coming suddenly to the writer, then an automatic setting down of an entire poem, story or part of a story. Elements comprising the creative process have occasionally been revealed in artists' own accounts of their inspired moments. Following an examination of these accounts will be a discussion of general theories of creativity to determine to what extent and in what manner the creative process emanates from the psychic process itself, rather than from a mysterious source 'beyond'. Finally, there will follow a discussion of the extent to which creativity is particular to human beings, not only to those possessed of special talents or aptitudes.

For Katherine Ann Porter, the stories seemed to "come" to her:

> All my senses were very keen; things came to me through my eyes, through all my pores. Everything hit me at once, you know. That makes it very difficult to describe just exactly what is happening. And then, I think the mind works in such a variety of ways. Sometimes an idea starts completely inarticulately. You're not thinking in images or words or – well, it's exactly like a dark cloud moving in your head. You keep wondering what will come out of this, and then it will dissolve itself into a set of – well, not images, exactly, but really thoughts. You begin to think directly in words. Abstractly. Then the

words transform themselves into images. By the time I write the story my characters are up and alive and walking around and taking things into their own hands. They exist independently inside my head as you do before me now [to interviewer].[55]

In this example, we begin to catch glimpses of the dynamics of the advent of the inspiration. Henry Miller begins to outline some of the requisites for the receiving of inspiration:

Yes, of course, there's something inside me that takes over. Who writes the great books? It isn't we who sign our names. What is an artist? He's a man who has antennae, who knows how to hook up to the currents which are in the atmosphere, in the cosmos; he merely has the facility for hooking on, as it were. Who is original? Everything that we are doing, think, exists already, and we are only intermediaries, that's all, who make use of what is in the air...[56]

...Thus, whatever effects I may obtain by technical device are never the mere results of technique, but the very accurate registering by my seismographic needle of the tumultuous, manifold, mysterious and incomprehensible experiences which I have lived through again, differently, perhaps even more tumultuously, more mysteriously, more incomprehensibly.[57]

Psychologist Frank Barron[58] has shown creative writers as a group to be unusually open to feelings of awe, despair, devastation, oneness with the universe, mystical communion, premonition, divination, etc. Tested on the MMPI (Minnesota Multiphasic Personality Inventory), distinguished writers score particularly high on schizoid, depressive, hysterical, and psychopathic scales, but they score high on prediction of recovery from neurosis, indicating their strength of ego. In other words, these are generally more sensitive people and have, perhaps, more going on psychologically; but if they are more troubled, they have greater resources with which to deal with their 'troubles.'

Creative insights frequently occur during a kind of trance state. As Goethe recounts the coming into being of certain of his poems,

> I had no picture of them, no advance idea; they fell unexpectedly into my mind and wanted to be set down at once, so that my impulse was to jot them down wherever I found myself, instinctively and as though in a dream. In this somnambulistic state, I often had the experience of finding a piece of paper lying any which way before me, of realizing this only when everything was written, or when there was no more room on the paper.[59]

Many poets have described creative inspiration in terms of inebriation, or somnambulism and lucidity – a lucidity, however, directed toward the subjective world rather than the outside world. Henri Gheon tried one day to work on an idea for a play but could come up with nothing; then, all at once, two months later, the following happened:

I was in bed, about five in the morning, completely awake, alert ... and clearheaded to the point of drunkenness, if there is no contradiction between those words. Everyone has experienced such a state, when you feel capable of thinking up the world. All at once, the tragedy of Saint-Maurice came into my mind, complete with all its characters, its intrigue, each act, each scene in order... yes, I was writing as though under the dictation of some other person.[60]

These 'inspired' moments occur to those who are extremely sensitive to the promptings from their unconscious and whose imagination is highly developed. When the two qualities fuse, their artistic gift pours out as if they were being spoken to by some outside force. Goethe was such a man; he wrote his poetry as it "came" to him:

It was, on the whole, not in my line, as a poet, to strive to embody anything abstract. I received in my mind impressions, and those of a sensuous, animated, charming, varied hundredfold kind, just as a lively imagination presented them; and I had, as a poet, nothing more to do than artistically to round off and elaborate such views and impressions, and by means of a lively representation to bring them forward that others might receive the same impression in hearing or reading my representation of them.[61]

The Fruit of Sustained Effort

Intuition and inspiration artistically manifested come not merely from these special moments. Writers generally must devote considerable mental attention and effort to the project at hand. Then, when the normal mind has exhausted its powers, intuition takes over. Aldous Huxley said,

> Fiction is the fruit of sustained effort...
>
> ...To write fiction, one needs a whole series of inspirations about people in an actual environment, and then a whole lot of hard work on the basis of those inspirations.[62]

The inspiration and creative flow of ideas comes within the area of focus of the particular artist. If the artist turns his attention and concentration to a particular mode or subject, he may accumulate sense impressions or information, until he feels a fullness within. For writers to sustain the imagination and keep it stirring and fully at work, in short, to manufacture inspiration, according to Roger Garrison,

> ...you need hard and productive thinking. Press your mind to be incessantly curious. Why? Why? Until relationships appear, sources are uncovered, motives are revealed, probabilities are envisioned. Day after day press yourself with restless curiosity to think in terms of images, pictures, probabilities, motives and drama.[63]

THE ABILITY TO SURRENDER

After the sustained effort has been put forth, the creator must allow himself to return to a more primitive stage of consciousness – to a condition of complete suspense, in which nothing tends toward determination, nothing seems to be implied. The artist must await the resolution of all the bits of information which have been held in suspension. One writer describes this moment as follows:

> Creation begins typically with a vague, even a confused excitement, some sort of yearning, hunch, or other pre-verbal intimation of approaching or potential resolution... Stephen Spender's expression is exact: 'a dim cloud of an idea which I feel must be condensed into a shower of words.'[64]

It is a fear of this stage of complete indecision that keeps many people from experiencing their creativity. They perceive this pre-verbal stage as being chaotic and disordered, rather than as an indeterminate fertility.

That part of the mind which is not verbal, linear, logical, does, however have ordering principles, although they are different from those of the verbal, linear functions of the mind. Arthur Koestler describes this order thus:

> ...Primitive phylogenetic tendencies towards rhythm and stylization with elemental violence; the emergent images acquire in the very act of birth a regular form and symmetry.[65]

In other words, the non-verbal, non-linear processes of the mind have a tension and dynamism of their own, which dynamism includes tendencies and drives toward resolutions at higher levels.

John Keats called the ability to surrender to these processes "the negative capability," that is, the ability to know how to exist in the midst of uncertainties, of mysteries and doubts, without the irritating desire to get back at any cost to the land of facts and of reason:

> The negative capability is the gift of remaining faithful to an intuitive certitude which reason rejects and which common sense does not admit; of keeping to a mode of thought which can only seem unreasonable and illogical, but which from a more profound point of view can reveal itself as superior to reason and transcending the logic of conceptual thought.[66]

When one yields to this "surging chaos of the unexpressed," as John Livingston Lowes put it, one can invent. To yield means to allow a diminishing of conscious faculties and of attention to external stimuli. One then slips into a dreamlike state, in which one is capable of listening to the poetic message. Ranier Maria Rilke describes it like this:

> I have always written very quickly, in some way subject to a rhythm that was seeking through me its living form. When this movement is in us, expression becomes just a matter of obedience. In this way, I wrote Cornet in just one night, reproducing effortlessly the images cast by the reflection of the setting sun on the clouds that I watched passing before my open window. Many of my New Poems have more or less written themselves, sometimes in a single day, in their definitive form. When I was

writing *The Book of Hours*, I had the impression, so easy had it been to begin, that I might never stop writing.[67]

By now it may be seen, from the foregoing examples of the occurrence of inspiration, that its source is not something Divine, it does not come from "out there somewhere." The source of inspiration is the individual's relation to the world. As Goethe said,

> ...you can never want occasions for poems; but they must all be occasional poems; that is to say, reality must give both impulse and material for their production... I attach no value to poems snatched out of the air... Reality must give the motive, the points to be expressed and kernel, but to work out of it a beautiful, animated whole, belongs to the poet.[68]

But once situated within "reality", the full depth and potential of imagination cannot be pinned down, for it is always bound up with history, with the evolution of humanity. Goethe was aware of this also:

> People are always talking about originality, but what do they mean? As soon as we are born, the world begins to work upon us, and this goes on to the end. And, after all, what can we call our own except energy, strength, and will? If I could give an account of all that I owe to great predecessors and contemporaries, there would be but a small balance in my favor.
>
> ...We live in a time in which so much culture is diffused that it has communicated itself, as it were, to the

atmosphere which a young man breathes. Poetical and philosophic thoughts live and move within him, he has sucked them in with his very breath, but he thinks they are his own property, and utters them as such. But after he has restored to the time what he has received from it, he remains poor. He is like a fountain which plays for a while with the water with which it is supplied, but which ceases to flow as soon as the liquid treasure is exhausted.[69]

Goethe seems here to imply limitations to the imagination, to suggest that imagination and inspiration are tied to objective "reality," external cultural and environmental sources. This is consistent with classical notions of the sources of art: the role of artist or poet was merely to interpret and articulate an objective reality, the nature of which everyone agreed about. A seminal figure in German Romanticism, it was Goethe who also challenged the traditional notions of reality, and posited a subjective or perceptual component to 'reality'. He even went as far as to suspect the existence of a sort of collective unconscious – a connection among men at the level of the unconscious. In speaking to Eckerman about certain experiences of telepathic premonitions, Goethe states,

There are many such things in nature, though we do not have the right key to them. We all walk in mysteries. We do not know what is stirring in the atmosphere that surrounds us, nor how it is connected with our own spirit. So much is certain – that at times we can put out the feelers of our soul beyond its bodily limits; and a presentiment, an actual insight into the immediate future, is accorded to it.[70]

Romantic poets such as Baudelaire and Wordsworth were haunted by notions of the existence of another world, that there were correspondences between the human 'soul' and nature. One of the more clear expressions of this presentiment is seen in this poem by Baudelaire:

CORRESPONDENCES

Nature is a temple where living pillars
Let sometimes emerge confused words;
Man crosses it through forests of symbols
Which watch him with intimate eyes.

Like those deep echoes that meet from afar
In a dark and profound harmony,
As vast as night and clarity,
So perfumes, colors, tones answer each other
There are perfumes fresh as children's flesh
Soft as oboes, green as meadows
And other, corrupted, rich triumphant,
Possessing the diffusion of infinite things
Like amber, musk, incense and aromatic resin,
Chanting the ecstasies of spirit and senses.

AUTOMATISM AND THE ORDER OF UNCONSCIOUS THOUGHT

It was the Surrealists who set about systematically to explore the process of unconscious thought as a way to discover the other world at which the Romantic poets had hinted. The Surrealists believed there to be a natural link between the personal unconscious and the collective unconscious, and the inspiration for their art (and later their political vision) derived from their perception of this 'reality'.

Their theory of the interconnectedness of humanity and nature was articulated as the theory of objective chance:

> As we are penetrated from every direction by electromagnetic waves which remain invisible and cannot be detected without the appropriate instrument, as we are shot through with innumerable electrical phenomena without our being aware of it, so are we also immersed from head to foot in the clouds and shafts of light of objective chance without our ordinarily being conscious of it. We are like the fairy-tale characters from a tapestry who, dreaming, forget that their matter has been woven on a loom and is only a picture placed in the tapestry.[71]

Hence, the Surrealists believed that telepathic networks united all mankind; we are all part of circuits of intermental [sic] thought. Then, we are never sure of being alone; literary inspirations perhaps come from another human being, linked by hidden affinities, who may never know that his message has been transmitted, according to the Surrealists. Andre Breton believed this interconnectedness had an immediately personal as well as collective meaning; the individual partakes of the universal:

> I am deeply convinced that every perception recorded in the most involuntary manner, as, for example, words addressed to no one in particular, carries in itself the solution, symbolic or otherwise, to a difficulty one has reached within oneself. One has only to know what direction to take in the maze. The frenzy of interpretation begins only when the man who is poorly prepared takes fright in this forest of signs.[72]

So, according to the Surrealists, works of art are products of collective inspiration; there is no strictly individual inspiration. Once again we come to the question of surrendering, of becoming receptive to the currents of social experience.

To cultivate receptivity to this hidden world, the Surrealists used the technique of wandering about the city (derive), or they found it in states of "mad love," or they put themselves into a type of trance state, in which they spoke or wrote 'automatically'. This is the technique of automatism, by which it was intended to express verbally or in writing (or by any other means) the real process of thought, without any control exercised by reason, outside of all aesthetic or moral preoccupations. To achieve automatism in writing, Andre Breton tells us the writer was to put himself:

> ...in the most passive, most receptive state possible and start writing without a preconceived subject in mind, rapidly enough not to be tempted to look back on what he has written. If silence threatens because he is thinking,

the writer is to stop and start again by putting down any letter, but always the same letter, bringing back the arbitrary by making that letter the initial of the next word.[73]

The Surrealists also believed there to be an order to the process of the unconscious, which was revealed largely through automatism:

> I maintain that automatism, in writing and drawing (without prejudice to the deep individual tensions in brings out into the open and even resolves to a certain extent) is the only mode of expression which gives entire satisfaction to both eye and ear by achieving a rhythmic unity, as recognizable in a drawing or in an automatic text as in a melody or a bird's nest. It is the only structure that corresponds to the non-distinction, more and more established, between sentient and formal qualities, and to the non-distinction, increasingly established, between functions of the intellect and of the senses (which is why nothing else can satisfy the demands of the mind to the same extent). In these unfathomable depths [of the unconscious] there prevails, according to Freud, a total absence of contradiction, a release from the emotional fetters caused by repression, a lack of temporality and the substitution of external reality by psychic reality obedient to the pleasure principle and no other. Automatism leads us straight to these regions.[74]

The Surrealists rejected the necessity of waiting for inspiration. Instead they affirmed the permanent presence of the interior message: the continuous discourse going on below the level of consciousness, to which one needs only pay attention in order to register it. When the discourse may seem discordant or incoherent, it still deserves the most intense attention.

But automatism does not mean unconscious writing. What Surrealism hopes is to immerse itself as deeply as possible in the uncontrollable processes of the subconscious, to throw out its net as far as possible, but still within the limits in which the consciousness will be able to take over and take lucid hold of the sunken treasures that are brought to the surface.[75]

The poet, novelist and playwright and self-described surrealist, Nanos Valaoritis has described Breton as writing "like a guided missile," or as using his conscious mind "like a captain guiding a ship through the shoals and reefs of the unconscious." [76]

Here, in Breton's poetry, is made visible psychic order, or poetic meaning, as it is allowed expression through automatic writing:

A MAN AND A WOMAN ABSOLUTELY WHITE

In the depth of the sunshade I see the marvelous prostitutes

Their dress a little faded towards the lamplight the color of woodlands

They carry with them as they walk a great fragment of wallpaper

Such as cannot be seen without heartache on the old floors of a house undergoing demolition

Or else a shell of white marble fallen from a mantelshelf

Or else a net of those chains which behind them become blurred in the mirrors

The great instinct of combustion takes possession of the streets where they stand

Like grilled flowers

Their eyes in the distance raising a wind of stone

While they stand lost and still in the centre of the whirlwind

Nothing for me can equal their unapplied thought

The freshness of the streams in which their boots dip the shadows of their beaks

The reality of those handfuls of cut hay in which they disappear

I see their breasts that place a point of sunlight in the Night's darkness

And the time these take to fall and rise is the only exact measure of life

I see their breasts which are stars on waves

Their breasts in which weeps forever the invisible blue milk

~ from *Le Revolver A Cheveux Blancs*, 1932

According to the Surrealist researches, what might appear to be the chaos of the subconscious processes is really not chaos, but rather several orders, or, as they put it, "numerous lines of force (champs) which convey the floods of images and of words and which fight for the attention of the consciousness." Thus there is always there is always the risk that automatic writing will change its content, or direction, or field or phase; it could resemble a succession of views taken by a movie camera that was being jerked about. The great obstacle, then, is not at all the lack of interest and of meaning in the magnetic fields of the mind which automatic writing explores, but, quite to the contrary, their super-abundance and the difficulty of tuning in to them perfectly.[77]

There is another kind of automatism besides the verbal. There is the continuous flow of visual images in 'the mind's eye.' The Surrealists, however, believed attention to verbal messages, or dialogue, to be the more sustainable source of poetic inspiration:

> ...Rimbaud and Lautreamont had no prior vision or enjoyment of what they had still to describe; they stayed in the dark antechambers of the being, listening to indistinct voices speaking, during the time that they were writing, of certain achieved or achievable things, without understanding them any better than we do, the first time that we read them. Illumination comes afterwards.[78]

The superiority of the verbal over the visual messages, according to the Surrealists, lies in the fact that the visual images are immediately reincorporated into the awareness as soon as they are perceived, while word-groups remain mysterious, that is, they do not immediately surrender their image-content to the consciousness, thus allowing the flow toward the conscious to be maintained.

Descriptions of the process of automatism would seem to guarantee success for anyone looking for artistic material within the unconscious. Indeed, the Surrealists asserted that the worlds of the imagination are not the exclusive prerogative of poets, and that all men(/women) have direct access to these marvelous regions through their own subconscious. Breton often affirmed the principle of equality for all men before this heritage:

> It is proper to surrealism to have proclaimed the equality of all normal human beings before the subliminal message, to have constantly maintained that this message constitutes a common heritage of which each one has only to claim his share, and which must immediately cease to be looked upon as the prerogative of a few.[79]

"Normal" here precludes not delirium, but rather the drying up of minds fossilized by utilitarianism, rationalism, (according to Carrouges[80]) as well as by the impoverishment of experience within the various alienations of producing commodities for the marketplace. To what extent automatic writing techniques can successfully be used to reverse gradually the process of repression required by wage labor and commodity production will be explored in the following chapter.

The heritage of the unconscious, more importantly, includes a language which is learned. So while Breton asserted that even if the images brought forth by automatism might be incoherent, the syntax would be correct. This can, however, only apply to those who have mastered a language and internalized that mastery. Language does not occur 'naturally,' and will not necessarily have a rich or coherent presence within the unconscious. The would-be automatic writer must also have a decent vocabulary and understanding of grammar. Herein lies the minimal role of intellect – automatism is not for those without some mastery of language.

For the Surrealists, automatism at first came without great difficulty. Practice alone was required to develop the facility for reaching at will into the unconscious or preconscious material. For many people, however, layers of repression and various compulsions and other neuroses get in the way of the flow or render the writer too fearful of listening to the unconscious.

But this process became more and more difficult for them over time, as with each excavation into the unconscious, they brought their discoveries – hitherto unknown symbolizations and relations among symbols and ideas – to the surface of consciousness. Gradually the conscious terrain became so cluttered with these newly conscious elements that it became increasingly difficult for the practitioners of automatism to break through the conscious level and plunge again into the pre- or unconscious. And gradually the Surrealists did run out of new relationships to discover within the unconscious, dominated as it inevitably is by culture.

And since the earliest practices of the Surrealists in the 1920's, the neurotic personality of our time has tended to change away from the model of simple repression towards the model of repressive desublimation as the socially accepted means for dealing with material which cannot be directly expressed within society. (Sublimation is defined as turning basic instinctual energy into a more "sublime" or refined expression or satisfaction; repressive desublimation is the inverse, in its repressive form.) So, whereas, the problem used to be that of unearthing repressed material, it is more often now the problem of freeing the creative impulse from its fetishized identification with what might be termed commodity hedonism: forbidden impulses are permitted as long as they are expressed as a libidinous identification with commodities, roles, or other products of the marketplace.

So the use of automatism currently has certain limitations. Nonetheless, automatism may be an important key for unlocking the creative process of those who are blocked by layers of repression as well as for those whose neurotic preoccupations get in the way or render them too fearful of listening to their unconscious dialogue. Specific applications of this technique will be discussed in the following chapter on Application.

THE INSPIRATION MODEL

For some writers, the necessary key to the unlocking of the subconscious process may be "inspiration". This approach is most often used by writers who have not mastered the technique of automatism.

The model of "inspiration" provides us with a more schematic perspective from which to view the "order" of unconscious processes. Inspiration is not always a mysterious visitation from places unknown (as in Goethe's speculations about telepathy), nor is it found only by attending to the permanent interior message, as the Surrealists affirmed. Often it is enough merely to notice inspiration: there are objects or experiences in everyday life which contain inspirational import. But what will contain inspirational import depends on the order of the unconscious, and the particular priorities of a given unconscious. The clues to the importance of the object or experience giving rise to the inspiration are revealed by 1) a disproportionate or even wholly inexplicable satisfaction or excitement which they evoke in the creative worker; and 2) their power to open the mind inward. What one in fact notices usually pertains to a missing piece or pieces of an incomplete gestalt, which is asserting a pressure for completion. According to Rugg, the incomplete gestalt stands out in ones perceptions:

> For the mere abstract idea of an incomplete pattern becomes alive of its own accord; it has a hole which must be filled, and this sets going the whole machinery of process, the valences of chemistry, and the attractions and repulsions of life.[82]

It is in order to complete the gestalt that we are compelled to select a 'figure,' according to gestalt psychology, from the undifferentiated mosaic of the visual field. We concentrate our attention on this figure, while the rest of the visual data recedes and fuses into a vague background of indistinct texture.

At any given time one may, however, have several incomplete gestalts, each clamoring for completion and preventing or making difficult the attending to of just one (just as in automatic writing, when the writer experiences the numerous lines of force which convey floods of images and words). For those incorporating a more conceptual level into their work and who are not ready or willing to plunge into complete automatism, they may resolve the competition among gestalten in a manner described by Anton Ehrenzweig:

> The artist may project all the fragmented parts of himself, incompleted gestalts, onto the page, or the canvas, etc. This must be done in an attitude of passive watchfulness.[83]

If the proper state of attention is maintained, that of a passive receptivity and spontaneity, combined with a conscious drawing upon the resources of craft and understanding, the artist may reach a state which approximates automatism: it resembles a trance state, characterized by a consciousness partly unfocused, attention diverted from the too-assertive contours of any particular schemata, and dispersed upon an object without complete schematic representation. This state differs from ordinary trance or hypnosis in its extreme watchfulness and its autonomy or self-containment.

The passive watchfulness is necessary in order that the unconscious may 'scan' the material to integrate the total structure through the countless unconscious cross-ties that bind every element of the work to every other element. The scanning reveals the art's substructure, but it may not necessarily heal the fragmentation of the surface gestalt.

Once the stimulus from the outside world is attended to and allowed to agitate the mind according to its own development, the expression or insight which will take shape will partake both of the ongoing imagery of the preconscious mind and of the secondary process of aesthetic judgment.

There is some disagreement among theorists of the creative process as to the location of the image process. According to Arnold Rugg,[84] the image process occurs at the level of the ordered, conceptual process of the mind, including the process of symbolization, the formation of metaphor, gestalts of figure-ground relationships, and the forming of judgment. The foregoing citations from artists concerning their own creative process, while not necessarily reliable, would nonetheless seem to provide some indication that symbol and metaphor, at least, have their origins in a pre-conscious level.

Sylvano Arieti[85] makes finer distinctions among types of imagery and types of process. He equates image and symbol, but says some symbols are primitive and belong to primary process, while others are high-level symbols and belong to the secondary process. For Arieti, the source of symbols/images is past perception; images are elaborations of memory traces.

The creative process traced from primary to secondary process, according to Arieti, goes like this: once the diffuse, disorganized, or primitive cognition from the primary process presents itself to the secondary process mechanisms, it may be adopted and used by an already existing concept or cluster of concepts of the secondary process. In the secondary process, aesthetic criteria, come into play and accept and/or reject materials, ordering them according to concept, i.e., the conscious identification of a relationship among the members or bits of data.

At the threshold of the conscious-non-conscious continuum, says Arieti, is where the illuminating flash occurs. A number of possible elements may be provided by primary process as solutions to a particular problem, but the correct element must be chosen by the secondary process. This is the moment of the illuminating flash.

For the automatists, on the other hand, it is more a question of listening attentively to one source from the unconscious, which presents its own order. For them, the recognition is sustained at a level between consciousness and unconsciousness, therefore it is not necessary to re-identify the appropriate missing element, having lost contact with the flow.

W.H. Auden wrote most of his poetry in the more consciously constructed manner, although of course some of his lines were "given." We see in his poetry a very different quality from that of the automatists. (Of course, Auden's style is derived from Anglo-Saxon modernism and partakes deliberately of collage rationalism, as opposed to the Spanish or French "associationist" poetry, which is more in the intuitive irrationalist style.)

Who stands, the crux left of the watershed,

On the wet road between the chafing grass

Below him sees dismantled washing-floors,

Snatches of tramline running to the wood,

An industry already comatose,

Yet sparsely living. A ramshackle engine

At Cashwell raises water; for ten years

It lay in flooded workings until this,

Its latter office, grudgingly performed,

And further here and there, though many dead

Lie under the poor soil, some acts are chosen

Taken from recent winters; two there were

Cleaned out a damaged shaft by hand, clutching

The winch the gale would tear them from; one died

During a storm, the fells impassable,

Not at his village, but in wooden shape

Through long abandoned levels nosed his way

And in his final valley went to ground.

Go home, now, stranger, proud of your young stock,

Stranger, turn back again, frustrate and vexed:

This land, cut off, will not communicate,

Be no accessory content to one

Aimless for faces rather there than here.

Beams from your car may cross a bedroom wall,

They wake no sleeper; you may hear the wind

Arriving driven from the ignorant sea

To hurt itself on pane, on bark of elm

Where sap unbaffled rises, being Spring;

But seldom this. Near you, taller than grass,

Ears poise before decision, scenting danger.

"The Watershed," W.H. Auden, August, 1927

The logic of the poem is constructed on a plane more removed from the processes of the unconscious; it is more linear, rational, although many of the connecting links between ideas and images have been deliberately excised. The sources of imagery come from a more sublimated reach of the imagination, where elements are condensed, distilled and juxtaposed according to a more conscious logic. The poem is doubtless beautiful; it is not here a question of judging which processes produce the most beautiful and satisfying works of the imagination. For many, however, the method of reaching directly into the unconscious is a more reliable method of avoiding the banalization and colonization by the dominant culture of the rational mind. The impulses emanating from the subconscious are more pregnant with hitherto undiscovered relationships. The imagery emanating from the more submerged levels of consciousness is fresher, more surprising and revelatory, than more consciously produced imagery and relationships, which have been kicked around as part of the social world enough as to be relatively more commonplace, not revealing anything new.

The final gestalt or completed arrangement of symbolic representations may not be arrived at always merely through automatic writing. If there is indeed an order, a unified perception, at the level of the unconscious, it, too, may be warped by various preoccupations or conflicts at some other level of the unconscious. In other words, blockages or distortions of the creative process may occur at many levels of the conscious or the unconscious systems. Hence, even many surrealist automatist attempts have produced only associations of images which are lacking in overall coherence or meaning. The focus of such writings might be upon the relationship between two images, or a linear series of images, rather than upon the whole. In this poem by Philip Lamantia, for example, occurs a syntactically correct arrangement of words, but the impact may remain superficial, unless the reader provides his or her own associations to the imagery. The poem may indicate that the creative process has been blocked at some level:

BECOMING VISIBLE

A whorl of happy eyes and devilish faces

struck out of antique sensuous paintings

twinkle from the knees and calves

moving slower than dream women

the hands are gesturing with violet blood

come from floating feathers

their sea-anemone fingernails opening tropical fruits

(mango skins, over snow)

and quickly rising to summer I meet you

walking in sateen boots over jewels of ice we spread

for you

With the fox to see by

subterranean rivers advance

from under an asphalt sky

Auroras you exhale

the scorpion poem between our bellies

the mint's pebble trickles down the

three thousand year old flute

washed up on a lemon-leaf bed

the way your look born of mollusk tears

mirrors the fins of memory in a dolphin's eye

Ah that taste of liquid spoon

magnified from the forest's apple

and where your odors

lie unfurling

comet's toes fire into

orioles (on their steps leave no traces)

twining my marrow's light

from your turning head of nervous lips

The stars dress up their furrows

whose divers sign you bathing

a torch of musk awakening my spark of fruit

~ Philip Lamantia, 1981

Though somewhat impoverished in terms of poetic meaning, this example of what we may call pseudo surrealism at least reveals more about the process of association of images than do most psychological studies. Among the latter, Sylvano Arieti's work is not incorrect as far as it goes, but it stops short of any comprehensive understanding of the process.

According to Arieti, the association of images which occurs at the level of the primary process follows the order of spatial or temporal contiguity. That is, images will be produced that were in spatial or temporal proximity with the stimulus of the previous images. For example, if I experience the image of a tree, that image will tend to elicit the image of other parts of the wood or garden where stands the tree, or of the landscape surrounding the tree, or of the people present at the time of the perception of the tree.

Or, according to Arieti, there may be a salient part of a perception, which may evoke other images which have the same salient part, for example, crescent, moon, and banana. Or, there may be a concatenation of parts that can easily displace one another, or a condensation or fusion of previous images that were separate in the real world, such as an image composed of half woman and half fish.*

Note: According to Paul Ray, latent thoughts undergo in automatic writing the same metamorphoses to become verbal that they do in dreaming to become visual: condensation, displacement, symbolization, dramatization, and secondary elaboration. Both imagery and words occur in the unconscious; it is a question of turning the attention to one or the other.[86]

To be sure, the process of association of images obeys laws of which we still remain largely ignorant. But Arieti ignores several dynamics of which we do know important aspects. Arieti sees only a two dimensional relationship of proximate or similar parts. While he accords some function to condensation, he fails to accord any importance to libido or desire in the process of the fusion of images in the imagination which were separate in actual time. Just as fantasy is the imagining of the fulfillment of wishes, so artistic imagery is an extension of fantasy and includes its component of desire.

The meaning embodied in a work of art is related to its expression of the individual's desiring relationship to the world. This includes some intuition of the artist's needs and wishes, of his own evolution as an individual. Any explanation of the association of images must include some understanding of the artist's framework of meaning.

4. For the Liberation of the Spirit: Perspective and Application

In the foregoing discussion (Chapter 3) of what inhibits creativity in the average person, some broad explanations were presented in terms of the domination of the subjective life by the culture of commodity exchange and the consequent alienation of human beings from the products of their labor as well as from their own subjectivity, the power of their perceived emotional needs, desires, imaginations and creative wills. The question remains as to whether the liberation of the realm of the subjective from the domination of the objective world, the world of the quantified, of rigidified roles and activities determined by the functioning of the marketplace is possible. If one assumes, as I shall, that the dominant culture does not exercise complete hegemony, then it may be possible to use the not-yet-dominated or subjugated remnants of human subjectivity towards such a liberation.

When no organized social movement is present through which to channel creativity directly into social transformation, one is left with recourse to more mediated forms of creativity, such as art (it might be argued that philosophy and science, and more dubiously, religion, are also mediated forms of creativity). However, when one of these mediated forms is used, there is no guarantee that the creativity involved will contribute to social transformation. The freeing of inhibitions to creativity through mediations such as art may go only so far as to enable the individual to more creatively adapt to his situation within the present system.

While the practice of therapy directed toward unleashing individual creativity is very preliminary and has quite some distance to go before the promises of social liberation may be fulfilled, there are, however, certain important accomplishments which can hereby be achieved. At this basic level, what may be accomplished is a significant restoration of the individual's sense of selfhood and potency, which are systematically denied by capitalism.

Lawrence Kubie's formulations are particularly useful at this preliminary level; the nature of the inhibitions to creativity in most people may be seen in terms of the "rigid anchorage at either the unconscious or the conscious end of the psychic system, preventing fluidity [of the creative] gathering, assembling, comparing and reshuffling of ideas." In 'creativity therapy', we see that those suffering from domination of the conscious system have internalized, generally at an early age, the values of the dominant culture, which form a rigid super-ego structure. These are the values of conformity to work discipline according to standards derived from the marketplace. Individuality and its creative expression have been subordinated to the ethos of competition. In school, the individual has been discouraged from expressing his uniqueness, and has even been made to feel guilty for not competing for quantitative measures of success, such as good grades. A child who might have expressed a talent for writing, for instance, more often than not will be praised for it only in the context of comparison with other classmates ("Isn't it great, Johnny, that you write so well. You're better than anyone else in the class.").

While creativity therapy may not be capable of creating a broad social movement to grapple with the problems of capitalist work relations in the marketplace, such therapy can begin to get at the roots of early conditioning for the submission of creative subjectivity to the dictates of capitalist work relations.

For those who fall into Kubie's category of domination by the unconscious system, the problem is the self-directed channeling of creative instincts which have escaped the conditioning of the capitalist work ethic.

A therapeutic framework which may be most generally applied toward the end of restoring a healthy balance between conscious (to include super-ego) structures of the psyche and unconscious structures and toward the fostering of liberatory creativity hereby made possible is that of art. Radical artistic expression, that which comes from the "root," can begin to integrate unconscious drives with conscious perception. The freeing up of and expression of unconscious impulses, through an artistic medium, can contribute to the liberation of the individual from enslavement to a super-ego dominated by considerations of the marketplace. The liberatory artistic expression, by cutting through the objectifications and dominant formulations of the market culture, may clear the way for the envisioning of a new social order. The following poem[87] by Adam Cornford illustrates:

ALIENATION

Cold word evaporating off the lips
the television says it is something enormous
a skyscraper with glass bones
a priest tells us it has always been
because God holds all the keys to our eyes
or: it is a tarry gas we find ourselves breathing
because we are
not trees, we are not ants or horses
or: it is a fungus growing on decayed marriages
or: it is a quartz pebble in the chest
that starts rolling around as soon as
someone else enters the room
I tell you it is none of these things
it is not a thing
but a motion rain sliding down a hair
an avalanche, a swirl of smoke
a movie running in reverse

It is the trickle of blood through the fingertips

into little invisible mouths

like the mouths of sea-anemones

they open in the keys of the typewriter

in the handle of the rivet-gun or the frying pan

they are small, they drink very slowly

you hardly notice as your veins

narrow into straw

your tongue becomes fiberglass and fills your mouth

your ears silt up with soot like old microphones

your skin rolls clumsily away

an old grocery bag under the wheels of a truck

After you go

the store windows gleam like newly-brushed teeth

the punch-presses chatter side by side

the cars wake up and breathe deeply

the bills caress each other in the cash-registers

they are in heaven where you put then

Alienation

to stop it you must stop the world

at first there will be a great silence

then a soft roaring will begin

a forest plunging its boughs into a storm

a complicated sound, a sound full of sounds

laughter machine-guns across a parking lot

children running down steel stairways

the rustle as factories are opened like books

as the pale ivy knotted around your spine

withers and falls away

and through it all

millions upon millions upon millions of voices

saying their first word

The liberatory work of art attempts to illustrate the reconciliation between the objective and subjective worlds. If this is accomplished, the perspective of domination may be reversed and external manipulations rejected. Through liberatory art, the artist reasserts his will and imagination to bring to light what he has hitherto been forced to repress and deny.

The question is often asked as to whether everyone is capable of artistic expression. Humanist psychologists such as Abraham Maslow give strong evidence, though indirectly, that everyone is indeed capable of some sort of creative expression. In his detailed examination of qualities of those Maslow deemed creative, he discovered the qualities to be those which are essentially human, theoretically potential in everyone. Maslow himself speaks of the universality of the "peak experience," the moment of intense creativity. According to him, while different kinds of people get their peak experiences from different situations,

> ...no matter where they get them from, the subjective experience is described in about the same way... It was a startling thing for me to hear a woman describing her feelings as she gave birth to a child in the same words used by Bucke (1923) to describe the "cosmic consciousness" or by Huxley to describe the "mystic experience" in all cultures and eras, or by Ghiselin to describe the creative process, or by Suzuki to describe the Zen satori experience.[88]

In his studies of self-actualizing creative people, those whose creativity derived more directly from personality than from special talent, Maslow discovered them to have in common a special kind of perceptiveness. These were people, according to him, capable of perceiving "the fresh, the raw, the concrete, the ideographic, as well as the generic, the abstract, the rubricized, the categorized, and the classified."[89] His subjects were relatively more spontaneous and expressive; their behavior was more 'natural' and less controlled and inhibited, with less blocking and self-criticism. They were free of fear or ridicule from others. Their creativeness was spontaneous, effortless, innocent, easy, and free of stereotypes and clichés. Maslow reports,

"Their innocence of perception and expressiveness was combined with sophisticated minds – they are relatively unfrightened by the unknown, the mysterious, the puzzling, and often are positively attracted by it." [90]

These are the traits characteristic of "fully functioning persons," as described by Carl Rogers.[91] If the manifestation of these qualities is used as an ideal measure of psychic health, we may interpret their absence as a symptom of poor psychic health, of blockage or neurosis. This is not to suggest that ideal psychic health is achievable within a repressive social order; this measure may only be used as an indicator of the degree of success of an individual's efforts to achieve a healthier relation between himself and his activity in the world. These qualities are not achieved in isolation from the problem of having to participate in the present social system. Creativity therapy may be used to enhance or develop these qualities, thereby strengthening an individual's capacity for sustaining a creative relationship to his world.

Not everyone will be capable of sustained creativity, just as not all neurotics can be "cured". However, every individual has a potential for creativity, which can be enhanced when the psychodynamics thereof are consciously understood by the individual. Moments of 'inspiration' which were described earlier, in the case of writers, poets, musicians and painters, happen perhaps with less intensity, frequency or duration in most people, but this does not mean that the potential is not there, not only for sustained creativity, but for social transformation as well.

WRITING AS A CREATIVE MEDIUM

Writing is an ideal creative medium in that it may be used not only to produce works of art, but may also be used in a therapeutic manner to facilitate the creative process. While great works of art are seldom produced without near-total dedication, writing can be useful at almost any level of skill or sophistication (although the plastic arts and music permit greater freedom of expression at pre-verbal levels). Through writing, for example, one can get in touch with and explore therapeutic issues such as hidden conflicts, preoccupations, desires and fears; one can discover possible resolutions to conflicts and outline plans for action. With the conscious shaping and externalizing, or expressing, of what has hitherto internal and not fully conscious, one begins to reverse the perspective of domination: one stops being a passive receptacle for externally imposed perspectives and begins to reassert desire, will, imagination, judgment. In so doing, one experiences oneself as a creator, which is the first step toward regaining a sense of oneself as a unique and potent being.

* * *

CREATIVE WRITING: THE BASICS

An examination of the process of creative writing provides a concrete model of how the creative process can be set in motion and sustained when there is no serious inhibition or blockage of the creative flow of ideas. The experiences here recounted by those whose life work is writing can be instructive to those who nay have no particular "gift" for writing, but who want to use the medium at some level for the expression of their own creativity. The problem of the removal of inhibitions or blockage will be discussed in the following section.

What are some of the obsessions that creative writers have in common? Creative writers have well-developed literary imaginations: they pay close attention to, are fascinated by, talk and think about people and situations, nuances of character and behavior. This is especially true of the novelist. The poet is more interested in metaphor and image. What both have in common is an obsession with words and language. In poetry the obsession with words reaches its purest form: every word matters. The writer feels he must write; he is uncomfortable unless he does write (and many writers feel uncomfortable all the time); he feels full, urgent with the need to make a good piece of writing. He feels that whatever keeps him from writing, however seductive, is temporary and of no great account.

And above all, the writer, professional and less-developed, must be open to his experience.* Henry Miller put it thus:

> [the artist]...has antennae, knows how to hook up to the currents which are in the atmosphere, in the cosmos; he merely has the facility for hooking on, as it were... I try to remain open and flexible, ready to turn with the wind or with the current of thought, to be flexible and alert, to use whatever I think good at the moment.[92]

Note: The following quotes are chosen not for their illustration of the importance of a "liberatory perspective," as earlier discussed, nor for the ultimate value of their literary products. They are here used merely to illustrate the more intimate dynamics of the literary process.

In such a state of openness, thoughts and perceptions will come, among which might be the seed of creation. Ralph Waldo Emerson[93] advises:

> Look sharply after your thoughts. They come unlooked for, like a bird seen on your trees, and if you turn to your usual task, disappear, and you shall never find that perception again. Never, I say, but for years, perhaps, and I know not what events and worlds may lie between you and its return.

Every day may provide a seed. One must to learn to notice that small occurrence, that slight event that is somehow out of resonance with the predictable fabric. Here's how Henry James described it:

> Stories spring from a "germ" – a single small seed, a seed as minute as and windblown as that casual hint for "The Spoils of Poynton"..., a mere floating particle in the stream of talk... The stray suggestion, the wandering word, the vague echo, at the touch of which the novelist's imagination winces as at the prick of some sharp

point: its virtue is all in its needle-like quality, the power to penetrate as finely as possible. This fineness it is that communicates the virus of suggestion, anything more than the minimum of which spoils the operation.[94]

The seed may be an object that comes to mind, not necessarily an immediate concrete occurrence:

> Often a poem is written with the eye intent upon an object that isn't there, before it. Such an object must be excitingly significant, capable of making the mind glow about it. Half the trick then lies in keeping the object spotted in the central furnace-light of the aroused excitement while the construction of the poem goes on in relative shadow, as if it were a thing of slight importance. For under these circumstances the structure may be played with freely and irreverently. Because the structure then never becomes an absolute, all the freedom of the mind's action is preserved to the last moment of the creative labor. To intensely imagine [the wader in the sun and slight of the coast] was therefore an important part of the process of bringing forth the poem.[95]

With poetry, the question of form can be at least as important as the question of inspiration. Baudelaire's work, for example, would be nothing without its formal perfection. It is the contrast between this perfection and the convulsive violence of the emotions expressed which gives his work its peculiar power. Form and content in art are always inseparable in the final analysis. This is especially true for modern art and literature. This poem by Baudelaire illustrates the point:[96]

THE CARCASS

The object that we saw, let us recall,

This summer morn when warmth and beauty mingle

At the path's turn, a carcass lay asprawl

Upon a bed of shingle.

Legs raised, like some old whore far gone in passion,

The burning, deadly, poison-sweating mass

Opened its paunch in careless, cynic fashion,

Balooned with evil gas.

On this putrescence the sun blazed in gold.

Cooking it to a turn with eager care

So to repay to Nature, hundredfold,

What she had mingled there.

The sky, as on the opening of a flower,

On this superb obscenity smiled bright.

The stench drove at us, with such fearsome power

You thought you'd swoon outright.

Flies trumpeted upon the rotten belly

Whence larvae poured in legions far and wide,

And flowed, like molten and liquescent jelly,
Down living rags of hide.

The mass ran down, or, like a wave elated
Rolled itself on, and crackled as if frying;
You'd think that corpse, by vague breath animated,
Drew life from multiplying.

Through that strange world a rustling rumor ran
Like rushing water or a gust of air;
Or grain that winnowers, with rhythmic fan,
Sweep simmering here and there.

It seemed a dream after the forms grew fainter,
Or like a sketch that slowly seems to dawn
On a forgotten canvas, which the painter
From memory has drawn.
Behind the rocks a restless cur that slunk
Eyed us with fretful greed to recommence
His feast, amidst the bonework, on the chunk
That he had torn from thence.
Yet you'll resemble this infection too,
One day, and stink and sprawl in such a fashion,

Star of my eyes, sun of my nature, you,

My angel and my passion!

Yes, you must come to this, O queen of graces,

At length, when the last sacraments are over,

And you go down to molder in dark places

Beneath the grass and clover.

Then tell the vermin as it takes its pleasance

And feasts with kisses on that face of yours,

I've kept intact in form and godlike essence

Our decomposed amours!

However the inspiration is arrived at, its sustenance is the greater problem. In the case of some works of art, the form itself contributes to the flow of ideas, due to their frequent inseparability. In other cases, what is most usually required is keeping at the task, continually keeping the imagination astir and fully at work; in short, inspiration must be manufactured. Honore de Balzac warns:

> If an artist does not sprint to his work as a soldier to the breach, if once within the crater he does not labor as a miner buried in the earth, if he contemplates his difficulties instead of conquering them one by one, the work remains unachieved, production becomes impossible, and the artist assists the suicide of his own talent...The

solution of the problem can be found only through inces-
sant and sustained work... True artists, true poets, gener-
ate and give birth today, tomorrow, ever. From this habit
of labor results a ceaseless comprehension of difficulties
which keep them in communication with the muse and
her creative forces.[97]

During this phase of the creative process, the rational faculties
must be re-engaged. One must remember what one knows, and
one must know a great deal about why a thing is, how it got that
way, what it could be in other circumstances; what are the relations between the things one knows? As previously mentioned
(Chapter 2), one must press the mind to be incessantly curious,
asking why?, until relationships appear, sources are uncovered,
motives are revealed, probabilities are envisioned. The writer must
day after day press himself with the curiosity to think in terms of
images, probabilities, motives, drama. After the vague perception
of the outline of an idea must occur, the reorientation of the mind
around the general story, then the gathering of observations and
thoughts, memories and associations.

After all the literary material is thus gathered, all the elements
of the story or poem (except in the case of automatic writing) are
put forth, there often follows a necessary period of frustration,
of bogging down. This period is the most exhausting as well as
the most profitable, for this is when the material is distilled, condensed and shaped. Out of it come pictures and insights which are
true products of the imagination.

During this phase is when many writers experience anxiety and fear of the unknown, when ego rigidity can prevent the work of art or writing from developing a life of its own. The unconscious fear of losing control underlies both. What the writer has projected onto the page during the phase of bringing forth material is often fragmented, mirroring the writer's own often fragmented personality. "Accidents" that crop up during the work can well be the expression of the parts of the writer's personality that have become split off and dissociated from the rest of the self. Ehrenzweig calls this stage the "schizoid" phase of the creative process.98 The writer must be capable of tolerating this fragmented state without undue persecutory anxiety; he must maintain the posture of passive watchfulness towards the work in progress so that his powers of unconscious scanning may integrate the total structure through relating the elements of the work to each other. Whence comes form.

During this phase the writer's receptivity to the workings of his unconscious is extremely important, as described by Tillie Olsen:

> Before the subterranean forces will feed the creator back, they must be fed, passionately fed, what needs to be worked on... [Then is a period of] receptive waiting, free from demands which prevent an undistracted center of being. And when the response comes, availability to work must be immediate. If not used at once, all may vanish as a dream; worse, future creation be endangered, for only the removal and development of the material frees the forces for further work.[99]

For the Surrealists, this phase was the most, if not the only, important phase. They cultivated the outpourings of the unconscious by deliberately placing themselves in a dream-like, or trance state. The intensity of the experience for them is well described by Francis Gerard:

> The exercise of automatic writing makes the subject undergo a set of sensations different from that brought on by any other kind of writing. Louis Aragon and Andre Breton had already compared it to the effect of those drugs that play on a harp with hempen cords. It is a fact that the person who lets himself be carried along by the rapid and uninterrupted flow of automatism soon displays an absolute indifference to his surroundings, and is plunged into an agreeable drowsiness which carries him further and further from external reality, bringing down between it and him a mist which the minds finds particularly pleasant, even though certain new sensations take on there an extraordinary sharpness and clarity. In this pleasant state, the body experiences a general numbness, with its life seeming to take refuge in a shifting inebriation and in an especially direct sense of invigoration coming from a completely inward activity. The very pleasant sensation might be compared to the intoxication produced by tobacco or, even more so, by opium. The mind moves through an opaque, vaporous region, brushing against its clouds like a perfume.
>
> If the writing is interrupted at this point, it will be seen that the eyes do not focus anymore on surrounding

objects, the legs are unsteady, the body exhausted; the mind experiences vagueness and a slight pain, the attention is disoriented and frustrated and is drawn toward the objects of lesser emotional content and of cruder matter that present themselves as obstacles. A sort of floating stupor blurs lucidity at the same time that it is carried along on a crest of pure exaltation and feverish activity that has been abruptly halted and left in painful suspense.

It seems that anyone who has often given himself up to this practice is unable afterwards to detach himself from it completely. Even between sessions, he is aware of this wooly feeling and of the fog hanging between him and the sharp outside world. He voluntarily retreats into this inner haven so that a subtle poison can once more open wide the doors, to a world where the mind can wander free in exultant freedom.[100]

The Surrealists took the products of automatism as finished products. In other types of writing, however, that produced by unconscious processes may seem to be rough and unfinished. And because this rough product, what Ehrenzweig calls the "undifferentiated substructure" [101] necessarily appears chaotic to conscious analysis, the subsequent stage of crafting the work is often beset with severe anxiety. During this phase, the writer must be accepting of 'imperfection' and work (and hope) for future integration. Tillie Olsen, again, warns against perfectionism, quoting Vincent Van Gogh:

Your work is unbeautiful. Alright, let it be unbeautiful. It will grieve you, but it must not discourage you. Nature demands a certain devotion, and she demands a period of struggling with her... It is the experience and hard work of every day which alone will ripen in the long run and allow one to do something truer and more complete. You will not always do well, but the days you least expect it, you will do that which holds its own with the work of those that have gone before.[102]

The final, or crafting stage, of the creative process, is a more fully rational process. The work is re-introjected into the ego, on a higher conscious level of awareness. During this phase, the writer's ego is enriched and strengthened. He completes the exchange between the conscious and unconscious components of the work as well as between his conscious and unconscious levels of perception. This occurs as the writer is re-writing, crafting the work into its final form, drawing upon conventions of style and grammar, making sure each word is the right word, rearranging, adding and subtracting, in short, editing. While this phase of the creative process is certainly as important as the preceding, I will not spend much time on it here, as the subject of this book is the source of inspiration and its cultivation.

BLOCKAGES IN THE CREATIVE PROCESS

Specific inhibitions of the creative process may occur at various levels of consciousness. On the most conscious level, hindrance may be due to distraction, failure to pay attention, lack of time, or conscious censorship. In these cases, the therapeutic approach may be behavioral or contractual. For instance, the writer who is distracted, who fails to pay attention, may contract with the therapist (or anyone) to make enough effort to notice the provocative events or things during the day that he may make a list of them and present them to the person with whom he is contracting. His agreement with some other person to do the work is often sufficient inducement to work for this type of writer. The first contract is then followed up with a contract to carry out the next steps of the writing project, such as developing one of the events the writer has noticed and been inspired by.

For the person who says he wants to write but has no time, the problem may be a simple matter of poor organization of time, or it may be a more complex problem of resistance – this person may not actually want to write, or he may want to write but has more hidden reasons for not doing so. In this latter case, a more analytic approach for uncovering hidden motivations may be needed. These approaches will be discussed further on.

The would-be writer with a conscious and explicit censoring of his own creative process is generally someone who merely needs encouragement. He may present his wish for approval or encouragement as a statement of his own lack of worth as a writer. Statements such as, "Oh, my stuff really isn't any good," or "I can't really write" must be interpreted in light of the context in which they are presented. In this case, when the would-be writer is talking to a writer's therapist, it may reasonably be assumed that he is at least interested in exploring further his ability or potential ability to write. Assurances given by the therapist, however, must not be made in the abstract, or they will be perceived as condescending and false. Genuine encouragement can be given only with reference to a specific literary accomplishment of the writer, be it ever so small an accomplishment.

When blockage of the creative process occurs at a less conscious level, that is, when the writer does not know what is keeping him from writing, the problem is then one of diagnosis as well as of technique for getting through the blockage. Those blocked at an unconscious level may present their problem as one of acute anxiety, the mind "blanking out," always having to get up from the typewriter to do something else, going snow blind staring at a blank page, obsessing over the appropriateness of a single word or phrase, or even as not wanting to write at all and "what-are-you-going-to-do-about it" (or, "I hate to write."). Diagnosis of these problems may proceed in a manner similar to standard therapeutic approaches used in diagnosing and treating neuroses, for a "block" to the creative process is, properly speaking, a neurosis. I prefer a therapeutic approach which combines guided free-association with specific techniques appropriate to the writing process. By guided free-association, I mean listening to the client, or blocked writer, talk about his writing problem while helping him keep on track with questions such as, "What happens when you sit down to write?", "What do you feel when you try to write?", "What does the block feel like? Look like?", "Can you describe the block? In a picture? As a person?" "Why do you want to write?", etc. These techniques will be discussed in greater detail further on with reference to specific aspects of blockage.

During initial phases of block therapy, as the therapist is listening to the blocked writer and beginning to formulate a diagnosis, there is one technique which may often be applied no matter what the source of blockage. This is the technique of automatic, or no-thought writing. Occasionally this technique alone is sufficient to dissolve a blockage, but at minimum, it is very helpful during initial formulation of diagnoses.

By automatic writing, here, we mean a less demanding technique from that practiced by the Surrealists. The blocked writer is asked to write non-stop, without "thinking", for ten minutes only. In avoiding the use of the rational mind, the writer in this manner may bring forth hitherto buried, material, preoccupations and relationships, as in psychoanalytic free-association. The level of rationality to which the writer may cling will reveal his level of inhibition.

For the seriously inhibited writer (but not including those who become paralyzed at the thought of writing), it is sometimes helpful to provide an extra stimulus to the automatic writing, something provocative to the imagination, such as music, an unidentified odor in a jar, a combination of incongruous objects (an umbrella and a sewing machine; a feather and a balloon).

THERAPEUTIC DIAGNOSIS

Diagnosis of the blocked writer's problem must include assessment of the writer's motivational structure as well as of the blockage itself. The two aspects are dialectically related, and their assessment may be made with increasing clarity in the process of therapy.

By motivational structure, I refer not only to why the writer tells himself he wants to write, which reasons may be superficial and/or distorted. If, for instance, a would-be writer tells himself (and the therapist) that he wants to write "in order to be a success," his desire to write will not have the strength and focus it would if that person were in touch with deeper levels of desire to write, or his own creative drive which seeks expression for himself as well as for others. Or such vague statements of motivation, such as the desire to be successful, may be covering up unresolved conflicts the writer may have about himself and his work, which conflicts may distort the creative process and bind up energies which might otherwise enhance the creative process. So the motivational structure includes deeper, often unconscious drives, including conflicts among them.

In exploring the writer's motivational structure, the therapist may examine first the more superficial layers, then peel them away, layer by layer, as the writer is ready to understand deeper levels of his motivation to create. In this manner, conflicts which have blocked the writer may be resolved, or, made conscious, they may be expressed in a creative context, thereby freeing the writer (ideally).

Diagnosis of blockage is usually facilitated by the clarification of the motivational structure. For instance, if someone wants to write in order to be a success in the eyes of others, it may then be determined in whose eyes specifically the writer desires to be a success. This may be a parent, or some person or group whose criterion the writer heeds more than his own. The problem can then be seen as that of the overweaning superego, internalized or not, which dominates the writer's own ego and/or libido

If a writer is blocked by some unconscious fear, then the diagnosis depends on revealing the motivation not to write. For example, as described in Case No. 1 in the following section, a woman I'll call "Connie", hated to write but didn't know why. What came to light during the course of therapy was that in school, writing had come to be associated with anger, which was overwhelming and frightening to Connie.

Less striking cases than the case of Connie usually involve fears of inadequacy largely, if not primarily, or guilt about creative impulses, both of which largely, of not primarily, derive from the internalization of the capitalist work ethic, in general. The sense of inadequacy about ones creative potential and guilt about exercising it is usually instilled during early education, and is reinforced daily when creativity is not only precluded from most work situations, but is also continually devalued by the culture, as has been earlier discussed in this book.

THERAPEUTIC TECHNIQUES

"SUCCESS STORY"

For a writer to imagine himself successful in terms of modern society is to begin to undo the programming for conformity to a culture of alienated labor and passive commodity consumption. When, in this technique, we ask the would be writer to imagine that he has written a best-seller, to imagine that he is a "success", we get him to begin to look at his own potential rather than merely to focus on his blockage, his failure. Within this framework may be revealed attitude the client's attitude toward himself in relation to society. This may include negative introjects regarding self-worth and ability, super-ego formations concerning external valu-ations to which he may be trying to conform, aid the motivational structure: why does he want to write?

In the "success story" technique, the therapist asks the would-be writer to pretend he has written a best-seller, and that it is in the windows of the bookstores. The therapist then asks how this has changed the writer's life. The response to this question may imme-diately reveal a motivation, such as the desire for "successful self-communication," which is fairly clear and straightforward. If the response is something like "I'll be rich and famous," the therapist must look deeper for clues to motivation, as there are countless ways to be rich, and other ways to be famous which are much easier than writing a best-seller. The therapist might at this point inquire as to the use the writer would make of wealth and fame.

Deeper levels of motivation may be revealed in the next step of "success story." The therapist asks what the writer's parents will say about the success of the imagined book, then what his siblings will say, his grandparents, his spouse or mate, a teacher. The answers to these questions also reveal the nature of the writer's support system as it might have been during the time his writing habits and attitudes were being formed, generally in high school. Herein may be revealed internalized demands for success or failure coining from parents and teachers, internalized parental messages dictating attitudes toward life and work, and, as is most often the case, internalized negative messages regarding the writer's ability, which continue to act as powerful discouragements to taking ones creative ability seriously (messages such as "Your spelling is terrible! What makes you think you can write?", or "Your grammar is all wrong. You'll never be able to write!").

From the information provided by the foregoing investigation, the therapist will be able to judge which psychotherapeutic techniques to next employ. For example, role-playing may be used to help the client act out unresolved scenes from the past between himself and parents or teachers regarding his ability to write (e.g., the unspoken response and dialogue with the teacher who insisted that neat handwriting was more important than ideas on paper. In re-enacting this scene and having his say, the client may reconfirm for himself that he was at one time in touch with his creative abilities and that they are to him more important than neat handwriting).

If the client is fearful of role-playing and/or is afraid of expressing very strong emotions such as anger at a person from his past, a technique which might here be employed is that of writing a letter which will never be sent. For example, a client may have so much anger stored which he had never expressed to the teacher or parent who discounted his work that he would be afraid to speak about it. Writing a letter to this person, telling him exactly why and how angry the client is, is a safe and effective way for the client to clarify his feelings, discharge them (or diffuse them) and be free of their troublesome aspects.

If the would-be writer has trouble recalling the situations which are the source of anxiety and which are unresolved, a useful technique may be that of guided fantasy. The client is instructed to relax, close his eyes, and to try to picture as closely as he can the scene or sort of scene he best remembers as experiences of pain or displeasure tied to writing. Wherever the client starts the remembrance, it can of itself lead to, or can be guided to, the scene wherein occurred the first significant discouragement to his writing/creative expression. Most people have no trouble remembering the general situation, which is most often high school English classes, and with guidance from the therapist can bring back into focus particular scenes, teachers, writing assignments, what the teacher said about them, etc. In "guiding" the client in his recreation of important experiences, the therapist employs basic principles psychotherapeutic listening, noticing what for the client seems to be "charged", suggesting the imagination of an action to break through a memory which is static, and asking the client to imagine what he had said, what he would have liked to have said (as in role-playing), how he feels at particular moments, etc. It is important in this technique to keep the client visualizing the past experience, so that it may be relived as a totality rather than as a half-conscious series of verbal messages. The visualizing and reporting of the experience may often be sufficient to complete unfinished gestalts and to make the client aware of his experience such that he may exercise conscious direction over whatever remains of the experience.

"HIGH SCHOOL HISTORY" EXERCISE

This is a more structured form of guided fantasy, to enable the would-be writer to recreate his past writing experiences. The structure of this exercise gives a sense of safety to one who might be too inhibited or too fearful to recreate formative writing experiences through visualization.

In "high school history" the writer is instructed to tell or write everything he can remember about writing during high school and while doing homework (such as where he did his homework, what the experience was like, did parents or siblings interfere and if so, how). This will inform the therapist of the general formative experience, from which information he may ask questions to reveal specific formative experiences. In this exercise, a useful technique may be to have the blocked writer list all the commands or writing rules taught him by his English teachers. These commands have usually been incorporated into the writer's superego to form a significant part of the blockage. They act as censors to the writer's creative impulses. The therapist will be able to judge the importance of these commands by the affective charge which the writer still attaches to them. The importance may be very explicit and understood by the writer, or they may be less conscious and require help from the therapist to bring their significance to light.

JOURNAL WRITING

This is a self-help technique that can be employed by any writer, for a variety of purposes, whether the writer is blocked or not, throughout the course of therapy or as a continual aid to the writing process. A journal may be kept on a day to day basis. It may be used by a writer who has trouble paying attention to his environment, to important stimuli. This writer might carry around with him a notebook in which he records, as they occur, striking or unusual events or things. These may be referred to later, as a treasury of seeds of inspiration. The writer who accumulates pages filled with writing will not be faced with the intimidating blank page when he actually sits down to write. This note-keeping may also include recording ideas and inspirations which occur at unpredictable times of the day or night. This technique not only builds up a storehouse of ideas, it also helps the writer learn to be attentive to his experiences as they occur.

Another use for the journal technique is to record the writer's attitudes toward his own writing. These attitudes may vary from day to day. The record of attitude changes throughout a week or two will give the writer an insight into how he relates to his writing, and will reveal patterns which can then be explored in greater depth. This is especially useful for the writer who, upon experiencing crippling negativity toward his work never goes back to the typewriter or writing table for fear that the only possible experience will be negative. If he can turn to his journal and read that he has also experienced positive feelings, he can reinforce himself to try again.

Another journal use is for the blocked writer to analyze his block. If each time he sits down to write he feels 'blocked', he may then turn to his journal to write a description of how the block feels, what it looks like. He may personify it: what sort of person does the block call to mind (see "Find the Critic," Chapter 5).

In personifying the block, the writer projects onto the page what have generally been unconscious components of either introjected expectations or commands from parents, teachers or peer group, or components of his own psyche which he has 'disowned', or not recognized as his own. In projecting these onto the page, the writer frees himself of their unconscious influence, clarifies for himself exactly what the influences are, and can then assume an active attitude of power over these erstwhile inhibitions. The writer, if need be, can proceed to write out a dialogue with "the critic," during which dialogues, the writer usually wins the argument with the critic.

* * *

The foregoing are techniques which may be applied directly to the writing process. Within the context of writers' therapy, however, any other therapeutic techniques appropriate to the releasing of inhibition in general may also be used. For example, for one client whose blockage resulted from, among other inhibitions, an extreme nervousness, I discovered that he never got physical exercise, and suggested that he do so. The general rule is, use whatever works.

5. Case Studies

CASE #1

A client whom I'll call Connie came to therapy when she had come to a standstill in the writing of her Ph.D. thesis. She had written and researched pages and pages but could not organize the material. This was the first complaint. My approach initially was to encourage her to discover the underlying organizing principle. This was primarily accomplished by asking her to tell me orally just what she wanted to say, what it was that interested her about this work, and why, after all, she was doing it. When posed these questions directly pertaining to her desire and interest, i.e., her motivation, she gave clear, direct answers, which contained the organizing principle – that which truly interested her.

After she'd discovered the organizing principle and we had drawn up an outline with which she was pleased, she claimed still to "hate to write." The source of the displeasure was brought to light with the "high school history" technique. I asked her to tell me about doing homework, to which she replied that she never did it at home, but just whipped things off in-between classes. When questioned about her writing experiences, she replied at first that she didn't remember, then recounted that at least one paper she had done was brilliant, but that the teacher had given her a "D" grade because of her poor spelling. The teacher had been very condescending and had made lots of red marks on Connie's paper. Connie was humiliated and furious, flew into a rage, and got sent to the principal's office. The mother was notified, came to the school, and said to Connie, "Oh, no! You'll be just like your father!" As it happened, the father was violent, frequently psychotically destructive and almost always frightening with his temper. Hence, Connie came to associate writing with psychotic rages, and ever since that time, "hated to write."

Connie appeared to be a very angry person, but she almost always exercised tight control over the anger, as it was too frightening an emotion in light of the father's example. We discussed anger, how frightening it really was, ways to let it out that would not hurt some 'undeserving' (as she put it) person, such as unsent letters, throwing pottery (on the floor), guided fantasy to complete incomplete gestalten pertaining to anger evoking situations.

This session was sufficient to get Connie writing again. After a couple of days she phoned to say she'd been writing, and that she'd also realized how angry at her spouse she was. This lead to other issues of dependency needs and of what to do after she'd finished her thesis.

CASE #2

A client whom I'll call Ralph came for counseling with the pre-senting problem, "I just haven't finished any writing projects. Something seems to be stopping me." Analysis of client's family and high school history revealed nothing which would explain his current difficulties. When asked to write what he would imagine to be the responses of his parents to having written a best-selling book, he reported that their responses would be predictable, sup-portive, and not very interesting. His affect toward family rela-tionships was flat, without any obvious charge.

Next I attempted to discover Ralph's motivational struc-ture. When I asked him why he wanted to write, he (in writing) responded that he wanted the satisfaction of having accomplished something. This seemed to be a valid, if superficial motivational impetus, so I then asked him what type of writing he wanted to do, how much he could expect of himself each day, and what he antic-ipated might prevent him from writing for the agreed-upon time period each day. I suggested that he do ten minutes of automatic writing in the event that he got stuck, but Ralph seemed to know what he wanted to write. He merely seemed to need feedback for his efforts and encouragement to write, more like permission to write, just for himself, rather than for someone else.

In view of his superficial needs – for encouragement and for someone "for whom to write," we made a contract, agreeing that Ralph would write at least one paragraph per day, on the days he didn't have to go to work. I instructed him to notice if he got stuck, to notice what he was feeling, at what point he got stuck.

At our second meeting, Ralph brought four pages of written material. He had not run into any blocks. He seemed more to want approval for what he had written, which I gave. Then we discussed a short story he had planned. He wanted encouragement to go ahead with the story and readily accepted my encouragement.

For our third session, Ralph brought two-thirds of his story written. He said he had gotten stuck and started daydreaming after having written that much. He and I discussed a couple of technical difficulties with the story, and he then worked out the rest of the story in telling it to me. He said that talking was easier for him, because he didn't have to be so careful. But, he reasserted, he wanted to write in order to think better of himself.

His comment about daydreaming prompted me to give him a homework assignment of making a list of his daydreams, writing about what he could or would prefer to do other than spend the time writing.

For the fourth session, Ralph brought his story, completed, typed. He brought no list of daydreams. Often a client will rebel against instructions to confront a block head-on, and will thereby avoid the blockage (as will be seen in client #3). But now Ralph brought up a more subtle form of blockage: he announced that he now wanted only to read books for three months, because, he said, "they're interesting." The clue to the resistance nature of this presentation lay in his statement immediately after that his writing was not interesting now. He had brought with him two samples of automatic writing, the first being rather stiff, the second more spontaneous and interesting. So I asked him to at least do fifteen minutes of automatic writing every day, to keep his hand in and to loosen up his literary conceptualizing.

At this point, some overall interpretation is in order. Ralph was an extremely nervous, person; he was painfully shy, didn't make friends easily, remained unassertive and lonely. These factors contributed to his need for an "Other" for whom to write, and provide the groundwork from which a strong transference onto the therapist could develop. What the client will heed from the transference relationship is self-validation on several levels: social, artistic, sexual (in the sense of gaining approval as a man). Ralph's extreme vulnerability resulting from his isolation and lack of sense of self worth, seemed to be contributing to the rigidity of his writing: his writing tended to be more in tune with his super-ego or with what he felt he "should" write, than with his sense of playfulness or creativity. His efforts at 'creativity' at this point consisted mainly in constructing extremely clever, complex plots with surprise endings, and in writing cute phrases of the type one might use at a cocktail party to impress someone very quickly with one's cleverness. What I felt Ralph needed was to really get into the automatic process, to subvert the rigidities of his super-ego, and to get in touch with his spontaneous sense of play. This should have had an effect not only upon his writing, but should also have restored to him a deeper sense of himself.

Subsequent sessions with Ralph bore out the truth of this diagnosis: he faithfully did his daily automatic writing, and his writing became freer with each exercise. I gave him strong positive feedback for the particularly good products of his automatic writing, which actually were quite good.

After a couple of months, Ralph again decided he wanted to write prose. He made several attempts, each of which produced a freer writing style; but he again ran into a 'block'. This time I asked him to notice the next time he got the 'block' and to write about it as a personification. The results were very revealing:

"FIND THE CRITIC"

A figure in a dark raincoat walks along the sidewalk, away from the trees. I can only tell that it's a male, my age or older, with enough shadow falling over his face to obscure his features. With his hands in his pockets, socks and shoes on his feet, and hat on his head, I see no part of his body: no skin, eyes, lips, or hair is in sight. He dresses in dark clothes.

This is my critic – always half a step away from me. By "half a step away," I mean that he has one arm, one leg, and half a torso, inside of my body, and the other arm, leg, and half-torso is outside of me. That is, he is partly occupying my self, and at the same time I am half-free of him.

Being half-free of him means that I can do some things some of the time. For example, I can think but not write, or begin to write for a few minutes but not be able to continue writing, or write well for a few weeks and then not at all for a long while.

His monochrome appearance corresponds with his absolute manner of blocking me. It's not very subtle: mostly it consists of whispering, "It's not going to happen," soon after I pick up my pen. Of course, for about twenty seconds after that, nothing happens. Then he adds, still whispering, "Well, now that you know that it's not going to happen, you can go do something else. And anyway, you tried." He follows this up by pointing out how uninteresting it would be to sit at the desk for the next twenty minutes or so and to have little or no writing occur.

The act of objectifying his 'critic' seemed actually to free Ralph from its clutches. In subsequent sessions we dealt not with blocks, but with the actual creative process itself. At one point, Ralph felt that his automatic writing was getting stale, slipping back into cliché. We discussed his level of awareness, of his ability to listen to the 'inner voice.' By reinforcing his confidence that the 'voice' was indeed there, I helped him be able to more easily surrender to it, to listen more receptively. His subsequent automatic writings were very interesting, but he gradually tired of the form and announced he wanted to write another story. I encouraged him to start from a 'seed' of inspiration, rather than to construct an entire plot meticulously, then try to fill in the characters and actions. This he was much more ready to do, and wrote the beginnings of a rather entertaining story, using an interesting blend of automatism and planned direction Ralph was very pleased with this story, but stopped after he'd finished the two pages, having gotten involved in some other activities during his free time.

When next Ralph called me for an appointment, he came without any writing, but rather wanted the personal contact. He told me he didn't want to write again for a while, and again wanted to read books. When I made a couple of suggestions about doing a little writing just to keep his hand in practice, he got angry with me and told me he was sick of taking orders. I accepted his anger as a healthy development of his transference onto me, indicating that he was working through it (having gone through the romantic projections a month or two earlier) and coming out the other side with more confidence in his own assertiveness. This latest outcome in his ongoing work with me is perhaps the most significant, as Ralph's major problem had been lack of confidence and consequent lack of ability to assert himself. He now knows that he can write when he chooses to, and that he doesn't necessarily need the 'Other' for whom to write.

CASE #3

The case of a man whom I'll call Michael illustrates the simplest form of behaviorist therapy. He overcame his writing block by making a series of contracts with me, some of which he complied with and some of which he contradicted, in what will be seen to have been therapeutic manner. Michael was a very bright, 31 year old graduate student trying to finish his Ph.D. dissertation. He had completed all his research, but found it impossible to write any-thing due to extreme anxiety upon sitting down at the typewriter. He would either obsess about the correctness of particular words, or decide that he had to get up to get something to eat or relieve himself.

Our discussion of his family and school history provided no new insights for Michael, as he had already analyzed all the fac-tors himself: he got excellent grades in high school English and continued to do well in writing in college, until his parents got a divorce. Michael characterized his father as a self-made success (who sells oil and gas pipes), who neglected personal relation-ships. Michael felt that his father would approve of his son's work, but Michael suspected there was a subtle pressure there. Michael liked his work very much (except when he got blocked). He had been somewhat estranged from his girlfriend during the past year.

Diagnosis: Michael seemed to have been accumulating anxieties from unresolved situations for several years. The lack of resolu-tion for such a prolonged period had resulted in a general vague-ness for Michael as to the sources of his anxiety; thus, he was paralyzed by what seemed to him to be general 'floating' anxi-ety. As he was scheduled to leave the area in one month and was seeking emergency help to get his writing going before he left for his week-long trip, an in-depth therapeutic approach was ruled out. Michael responded well, however, to the behaviorist contract approach.

The first contract agreed upon by Michael and myself was designed to make him accountable to someone else (myself). He agreed to write from 8:00 to 1 p.m. every day, to take three 15 minute breaks as his programmed 'avoidance' behavior. If he were to encounter his block, I instructed him to write about it, to dialogue with it. Last, if he ran into the block, he was to write what life would be like for him after he finished his dissertation (this technique was designed to probe more deeply his motivational structure). Michael came back in a week, saying he had been writing all week and had not run into his block. His avoidance behavior had been transplanted onto the assignment to write about the block, freeing him to write on his dissertation. Before his departure, he'd agreed that what helped him was having someone else to whom to be accountable, and that when he was away on his trip, he would find someone with whom to 'contract'.

This behaviorist approach does not pretend to be definitively therapeutic, it is merely expedient. I don't know whether Michael finished his dissertation, as we're no longer in contact, but it is possible that if he did finish his dissertation he would have enough feeling of accomplishment to attain some separation from the unresolved situations accumulated previously. Or it is possible that finishing the dissertation would have freed him to deal with his anxiety at a deeper level.

CLIENT MICHAEL WRITING FROM
SEED OF INSPIRATION

She was the first one I noticed after pushing open the coffeehouse door, and the only one I continued to look at. She was sitting by herself at a small table with a white laminated plastic top that held up her coffee cup, her purse, and her elbows. She was trying not to drink the coffee; this was done by pushing the cup to the farthest edge of the table and placing the purse between the cup and herself. She lifted her eyes after I had stared at her off and on for about half a minute. By that time I had noticed the effect on me of her shoulder-blade-length blonde hair against her violet knit dress and of her sole make-up, black mascara. As I returned to looking at her face, our eyes met and she exhaled phlegmatically out her nose. I then noticed her hands: reddened backs and rough fingernails; hands that had worked. I decided to approach this woman. As I walked toward her, her head tilted upward and her jaw fell down.

"I'd like to talk to you because I used to work here." It was the most coherent lie I knew.

"You used to work here?"

"Yeah, in the kitchen" – I sat down on the chair to her left – "and I thought I saw you here one time arguing with the boss."

"Me? With the boss? No. Wait – no."

It was a swell introduction, absolutely non-threatening, but with the obvious weakness of being non-sustaining after ten seconds. Time to think fast. Maybe say something about her hair?

"Well, maybe your hair was a different color then."

"No, I always color it blonde... Hey, wait a minute – if my hair was a different color then, why could you recognize me now?"

"Well, maybe I remembered the dress." I was so nervous my jaw was numb. She and I weren't working out too well. Better talk some more. "The purple dress," I said, pointing somewhat carelessly at her left breast. She drew back an inch. Watch it, I thought. She exhaled loudly through her mouth, looked away for an instant, then put a hand on her purse and looked hard at me.

"I've never been here before and what the hell do you want?"

I was paralyzed; I just wanted to get out of there and knew that I couldn't think of any kind of reply other than to say the first word that appeared in my mind. Out it came: "An eraser."

"What?" she half-yelled. "An – eraser?"

"Yeah, so I could get out of here," I said quickly.

"Why don't you just get out of here?" she replied, slightly shaking her head.

"Well, I would, except I've got to – instant word time again – 'measure an angel.'"

She gave me a disgusted stare. I decided to keep going along this line, hoping to gracefully extricate myself from this mess by appearing as an ordinary weirdo.

"You see, the planking needs to be shortened for the surprise...surprise of my sister, the chemist...she makes tungsten brownies that the boss...the boss...well, he likes them – but not her ...and so I have to petition the crying lord with the galley...vibratos...that tank their pleasure in the employment...shingles. You see, I'm unemployed."

She shut her eyes hard, then opened them at me. "Get out of here or I will."

I made a last attempt, an attempt at wit. "No, I will." She did not reply to that. So I stood up and quickly walked outside.

Conclusion

In the foregoing, I have loosely outlined considerations towards an adequate theory of the creative process. A new, more comprehensive theory must include an understanding of the psychodynamics of creativity, the function of the social context and the dialectical relation between the two. Concepts such as desire, meaning, social relation have here been left vague, as each concept requires extensive treatment, for which there is not the space in this book.

This book also does not include a treatment of the differences between the creativity of ordinary people and that of great artists or creative geniuses. The uniqueness of particular creative geniuses must, in the final analysis, be attributable to as many factors as compose the life of a single individual, inclusive of his historical period. Such an analysis would necessarily include physiological factors, biological, neurological, economic, political, sociological and technological factors. The purpose of this book, rather, has been to understand the ways in which creativity is part of human nature, and as such, accessible to everyone and even necessary to psychic health.

There remains, still, a large gap between the theories I have presented and their application. The application deals only with one limited application of creativity – the process of creative writing, and not with the infinite variety of possible creative outlets or media. While variants of the same dynamics of the creative process might well be applied to other forms of artistic expression, such as painting, dance, music, architecture, each application is sufficiently specific in its materials and practical requirements as to require specific treatment in any writing about them.

I have in this book only begun to touch upon the art of writing itself, and have dealt only with fictional and poetic writing, which I have felt could illustrate the more purely creative aspects of writing. And within this framework, I hope to have illustrated the basic principles of the creative process which night be applied to the understanding of the creative process through any median.

The application of creative principles here discussed has dealt primarily with the individual as he is able to withdraw from the forces of repression and fragmentation inherent in the capitalist organization of work, and as he is able to adopt the posture of artist. The artist in isolation from a broader social movement is limited in what he can accomplish toward the end of social liberation, the freeing of a society from the fetters of an outmoded form of social organization. At best, the writing of an individual can serve as a medium through which he can begin to express his own perceptions of the world, his desires, his vision of a better world, his understanding of what and how to change the present world. Writing alone does not social transformation make; the writer cannot exist independently of capitalist society until such time as that society is transformed into something else. The sine qua non, however, of social change, is the spark of individual creativity. Nothing progressive can happen at the social level without the efforts of individuals who take their desires seriously, and from that point begin to formulate visions of a new society. As Karl Marx put it,

> *Authentic common life arises not through reflection; rather it comes about from the need and egoism of individuals, that is, immediately from the activation of their very existence. It is not up to man whether this common life exists or not. However, so long as man does not recognize himself as man and does not organize the world humanly, this common life appears in the form of alienation, because its subject, man, is a being alienated from itself.*[103]

Footnotes

1. Marx, Karl, *Das Kapital,* v. I, (Moscow: Progress Publishers, 1965), p. 178.

2. Freud, Sigmund, "The Ego and the Id," in *A General Selection* (New York: Doubleday, 1957), p. 227.

3. Freud, Sigmund, *On Creativity and the Unconscious* (New York: Harper and Brothers, Inc., 1958), p. 47.

4. Pavlov, Ivan, Conditioned Reflexes: An Investigation of the *Physiological Activity of the Cerebral Cortex,* 1927 lecture, in Experimental Psychology and other Essays, 1957, (New York: Philosophical Library, 1957).

5. Arieti, Sylvano, *Creativity, the Magic Synthesis* (New York: Basic Books, 1976), pp. 37-52.

6. ibid., p. 297.

7. ibid., p. 237.

8. ibid., p. 413.

9. ibid., p. 313; 373.

10. ibid., p. 12.

11. Maslow, Abraham H., *Toward a Psychology of Being* (Princeton: Van Nostrand Co., 1963), p. 129.

12. ibid., p. 51.

13. Jacoby, Russell, *Social Amnesia: A Critique of Conformist Psychology* (Boston: Beacon Press, 1979), pp. 49-50.

14. Hegel, George F.V., *The Phenomenology of Mind* (New York: Harper & Row, 1967), p. 83.

15. Jacoby, op. cit., p. 52.

16. Kubie, Lawrence, *Neurotic Distortion of the Creative Process* (Kansas: University of Kansas Press, 1950), p. 1-52.

17. ibid., p. 54.

18. ibid.

19. Ehrenzweig, op. cit., p. 267.

20. ibid., p. 13.

21. ibid., p. 15

22. ibid., p. 272.

23. Breton, Andre, *Manifestoes of Surrealism* (Ann Arbor: University of Michigan Press, 1969), p. 38.

24. DeBord, Guy, *Society of the Spectacle* (Detroit: Black and Red Press, 1970), paragraph 186.

25. ibid., p.165.

26. DeBord, Guy, in translation by Christopher Gray, in *Leaving the Twentieth Century: The Incomplete Work of The Situationist International,* "Formula for a New City," (orig. Paris:1958-69); translation (New Zealand: Rebel Press 1998), p. 18.

27. ibid., p. 19.

28. ibid.

29. Seidel, George, *The Crisis of Creativity* (Indiana: University of Notre Dame Press, 1966).

30. Hardison, O.B. Jr., *Modern Continental Literary Criticism* (London: Peter Owen Press, 1962), p. 165.

31. Ghiselin, Brewster, ed., *The Creative Process,* (New York: New American Library, 1952), p. 165.

32. *Writers at Work: The Paris Review Interviews,* second series (New York: Viking Press, 1963), p. 151.

33. Ghiselin, op. cit., p. 199.

34. Delgado, Jose, "Manipulation of Behavior by Direct Stimulation of the Brain," paper presented at the Columbia University Seminars on Technology and Social Change, Nov. 1966, mimeo, p. 19, cited in Hampden-Turner, Charles, *Radical Man,* (New York: Anchor Books, 1971), p. 25.

35. Lukacs, *History and Class Consciousness* (Cambridge: MIT Press, 1971), p. 83.

36. Braverman, Harry, *Labor and Monopoly Capital,* especially Chapter 4, "Scientific Management."

37. Lukacs, ibid., p. 89.

38. Perls, Fritz, Hefferline & Goodman, *Gestalt Therapy* (New York: Dell Publishing, 1951), p. ix.

39. Jacoby, Russell, op. cit., p. 4.

40. Marcus, Lyn, *Dialectical Economics* (Lexington: D.C. Heath & Co., 1975), p. 98.

41. Horkheimer, Max, *Critical Theory* (New York: Herder & Herder, 1972), p. 277.

42. Marcuse, Herbert, *The Aesthetic Dimension* (Boston: Beacon Press, 1977), p. 44.

43. Breton, op. cit.

44. Carrouges, Michael, *Andre Breton and the Basic Concepts of Surrealism* (Alabama: University of Alabama Press, 1974), p. 11.

45. Breton, Andre, in *What is Surrealism,* edited by Rosemont, Franklin (London: Pluto Press, 1978), p. 129.

46. Marcuse, op. cit, p. 7.

47. Miller, Henri, cited in Ghiselin, op. cit., p. 181.

48. DeBord, Guy, *Society of the Spectacle,* op. cit., paragraph 191.

49. DeBord, Guy, in *Leaving the Twentieth Century,* op. cit.

50. DeBord, Guy, ibid., "The Construction of Situations," p. 1.

51. ibid.

52. DeBord, Guy, in *Leaving the Twentieth Century,* ibid.

53. Cobb, Stanwood, *The Importance of Creativity* (Netuchen, N.J.: Scarecrow Press, 1967), p. 93.

54. ibid.

55. *Paris Review Interviews,* op. cit., p. 51.

56. ibid., p. 172.

57. Ghiselin, op. cit., p. 182.

58. Barron, Frank, *Creativity and Psychological Health* (Princeton, N.J.: Van Nostrand, 1963).

59. Carrouges, op. cit., p. 112.

60. ibid., p. 27.

61. Hardison, op. cit., p. 50.

62. Cobb., op. cit., p. 94.

63. Garrison, Roger H., *A Creative Approach to Writing* (New York: Holt, 1951).

64. Ghiselin, op. cit. p. 119.

65. Koestler, Arthur, *The Act of Creation* (London: Hutchinson & Co., 1964)

66. Carrouges, op. cit., p. 73.

67. ibid., p. 113.

68. Hardison, op. cit. p. 51.

69. ibid.

70. Carrouges, op. cit., p. 198.

71. ibid., p. 199

72. ibid., p. 259.

73. Ray, Paul C., *The Surrealist Movement in England* (London: Cornell University Press, 1971), p. 8

74. Rosemont, Franklin, *Andre Breton: What is Surrealism?* (London: Pluto Press, 1978) p. 217.

75. ibid.

76. Valaoritis, Nanos, private conversation, 1980.

77. Carrouges, op. cit., p. 137.

78. ibid., p. 135.

79. ibid.

80. Carrouges, ibid.

81. Marcuse, *One Dimensional Man,* (Boston: Beacon Press), 1968.

82. Rugg, Harold, *Imagination* (New York: Harper & Row, 1963), p. 302.

83. Ehrenzweig, Anton, *The Hidden Order of Art* (Berkeley: University of California Press, 1967), p. 102.

84. Rugg, op. cit.

85. Arieti, op. cit., p. 37-52.

86. Ray, op. cit., p. 7.

87. Cornford, Adam, *Shooting Scripts,* (Missoula: Blackstone Press), 1973.

88. Maslow, op. cit., p. 69.

89. ibid., p. 129.

90. ibid., p. 130.

91. Rogers, Carl R., *On Becoming a Person* (Cambridge: Riverside Press, 1961), p. 183 ff.

92. *Writers at Work: The Paris Review Interviews,* op. cit., p. 172.

93. Ralph Waldo Emerson, *Journals & Miscellaneous Notebooks of Ralph Waldo Emerson,* Cambridge: Belknap Press of Harvard University Press 1973.

94. Ghiselin, op. cit., p. 147.

95. ibid., p. 128.

96. Baudelaire, Charles, in *The Penguin Book of Modern Verse Translation* (England: Penguin Books, 1966), p. 159.

97. Graham, John, *Craft So Hard to Learn; Conversations with Poets and Novelists* (New York: Morrow Paperback Editions, 1972).

98. Ehrenzweig, op. cit., p. 102.

99. Olsen, Tillie, *Silences* (New York: Dell Publishing Co., 1978), p. 157.

100. Carrouges, op. cit., p. 129.

101. Ehrenzweig, op. cit. p. 37 ff.

102. Olsen, op. cit.

103. Marx, Karl, "Money and Alienated Man," in Easton and Guddat, *Writings of the Young Marx on Philosophy and Society,* Garden City: Doubleday, p. 272.

Bibliography

Anderson, Harold H., ed., *Creativity and its Cultivation,* New York: Harper & Row, 1959.

Arieti, Sylvano, Creativity, *The Magic Synthesis,* New York: Basic Books, 1976.

Arnheim, Rudolf, *Art & Visual Perception: A Psychology of the Creative Eye,* Berkeley: University or California, 1974.

Barfield, Owen, *Poetic Diction: A Study in Meaning,* New York: McGraw Hill, 1964.

Barren, Frank, *Creativity and Psychic Health.* Princeton, N.J.: Van Nostrand, 1963.

Benjamin, Walter, *Reflections,* New York: Harcourt Brace Jovanovich, Inc., 1978.

Bergler, Edmund, *The Writer and Psychoanalysis.* New York: Doubleday, 1950.

Boorstin, Daniel J., *The Image: A Guide to Pseudo-Events in America.* New York: Atheneum Press, 1975.

Braverman, Harry, *Labor and Monopoly Capital,* Monthly Review Press; December 1, 1998.

Breton, Andre, *Manifestoes of Surrealism,* Ann Arbor: University of Michigan Press, 1969.

Carrouges, Michel, A*ndre Breton and the Basic Concept s of Surrealism.* Alabama: U of A

Cauldwell, Christopher, *Illusion and Reality,* New York: International Publishers, 1973.

Cobb, Stanwood, *The Importance of Creativity,* New Jersey: Scarecrow Press, 1967. ed.

Cornford, Adam, *Shooting Scripts,* Missoula: Blackstone Press, 1973.

Debord, Guy, *Internationale Situationiste,* Paris, 1958-69.

_____ *The Society of the Spectacle,* Detroit: Black and Red Press, 1970.

Ehrenzweig, Anton, *The Hidden Order of Art: A. Study in the Psychology of Artistic Imagination,* Berkeley: University of California Press, 1967.

Enzensberger, Hans Magnus, *The Consciousness Industry; On Literature, Politics, and the Media,* New York: Seabury Press, Inc., 1974.

Fenichel, Otto, *The Psychoanalytic Theory of Neurosis.* New York: W.W. Norton & Co., 1945.

Freud, Sigmund, *The Basic Writings of Sigmund Freud,* ed. by A.A. Brill, New York: The Modern Library (Random House), 1938.

_____ *A General Selection,* edited by John Rickman, New York: Doubleday, 1957.

_____ *Leonardo Da Vinci and a Memory of His Childhood,* New York: W.W. Norton & Co., Inc., 1964.

_____ *On Creativity and the Unconscious,* New York: Harper & Brothers, Inc., 1958.

Garrison, Roger H. *A Creative Approach to Writing,* N.Y.: Holt, 1951.

Ghiselin, Brewster, ed. *The Creative Process,* New York: New American Library, 1952.

Graham, John, *Craft So Hard to Learn: Conversations with Poets and Novelists about the Teaching of Writing.* New York: Morrow Paperback Editions, 1972.

Hampden-Turner, Charles, *Radical Man.* New York: Anchor Books, 1971.

Hardison, O.B. Jr., ed., *Modern Continental Literary Criticism.* London: Peter Owen, 1962.

Hauser, Arnold, *The Social History of Art,* New York: Vintage Books, 1960.

Hegel, George W.F., *The Phenomenology of Mind,* New York: Harper & Row, 1967.

Horkheimer, Max, *Critical Theory,* New York: Herder & Herder, 1972.

Horkheimer, Max, & Adorno, Theodore, *Dialectic of Enlightenment,* New York: Herder & Herder, 1972.

Jacoby, Russell, Social Amnesia: *A Critique of Conformist Psychology from Adler to Laing,* Boston: Beacon Press, 1979.

Jay, Martin, *The Dialectical Imagination,* Boston: Little, Brown & Co., 1973

Kagan, Jerome, ed., *Creativity and Learning,* Boston: Beacon Press, 1967.

Koestler, Arthur, *The Act of Creation,* London: Hutchinson & Co., 1964.

Kris, Ernst, *Psychoanalytic Explorations in Art,* New York: International Universities Press, 1962.

Kubie, Lawrence S., *Neurotic Distortion of the Creative Process,* Kansas: University of Kansas Press, 1950.

Lasch, Christopher, *Haven in a Heartless World: The Family Besieged,* New York: Basic Books, Inc., 1977.

Lukacs, Georg, *History and Class Consciousness: Studies in Marxist Dialectics,* Cambridge: M.I.T. Press, 1971.

Braverman, Harry, *Labor and Monopoly Capital,* 1974 (first edition) New York: Monthly Review Press, 1998.

Mack, Karin and Skjei, Eric, *Overcoming Writing Blocks,* Los Angeles: J.P. Tarcher, Inc., 1979.

Marcus, Lyn, *Dialectical Economics,* Lexington, Toronto, London: D.C. Heath & Co., 1975.

Marcuse, Herbert, *Eros and Civilization,* New York: Vintage Books, 1962.

_____*The Aesthetic Dimension: Toward a Critique of Marxist Aesthetics,* Boston: Beacon Press, 1977.

_____Lectures, Boston: Beacon Press, 1970.

Marx, Karl, *Das Kapital,* vol. I, p. 178, Moscow, 1965.

Marx, Karl, "Money and Alienated Man," Easton and Guddat, *Writings of the Young Marx on Philosophy and Society.* Garden City: Doubleday, 1967.

Maslow, Abraham H., *Toward a Psychology of Being,* Princeton: Van Nostrand Co., 1962.

May, Rollo, *The Courage to Create,* New York: Bantam Books, 1975.

Nicholi, Armand M., Jr., ed., *Harvard Guide to Modern Psychiatry.* Cambridge: Belknap Press, 1978.

Norman, Charles, ed., *Poets on Poetry,* New York: Collier Books, 1962.

Olsen, Tillie, *Silences,* New York: Dell Publishing Co., 1978.

Perls, Frederick S., *Gestalt Approach and Eyewitness to Therapy,* Palo Alto: Science and Behavior Books, Inc., 1973.

Perls, Frederick S., Hefferline, Ralph F., and Goodman, Paul, *Gestalt Therapy,* New York: Bantam Books; Bantam Edition, 1977.

Paris Review Interviews, *Writers at Work,* New York: Viking Press, 1963.

Progoff, Ira, *At a Journal Workshop: The Basic Text and Guide for Using the Intensive Journal,* New York: Dialogue House Library, 1976.

Rainer, Tristine, *The New Mary,* Los Angeles: J.P. Tarcher, Inc., 1978.

Ray, Paul C., *The Surrealist Movement in England,* London: Cornell University Press, 1971.

Rogers, Carl R., *On Becoming a Person,* Boston: Houghton Mifflin Co., 1961.

Rosemont, Franklin, ed., *Andre Breton: What is Surrealism,* London: Pluto Press, 1978.

Rosner, Stanley and Abt, Lawrence, eds., *Essays in Creativity,* New York: North River Press, Inc., 1974.

Rugg, Harold, *Imagination,* New York: Harper & Row, 1963.

Ruitenbeek, Hendrik M., ed., *The Creative Imagination; Psychoanalysis and the Genius of Inspiration,* Chicago: Quadrangle Books, 1965.

Sartre, Jean-Paul, *The Psychology of Imagination,* New York: Philosophical Library, 1948.

Sealts, Merton M. Jr. *Journals & Miscellaneous Notebooks of Ralph Waldo Emerson,* Cambridge: Belknap Press of Harvard University Press 1973

Seidel, George, *The Crisis of Creativity,* Indiana: University of Notre Dame Press, 1966.

Tillett, Nettie S., *How Writers Write: Essays by Contemporary Authors,* New York: Thomas Y. Crowell., 1937.

About the Author

Karen McChrystal, M.A., is an author and interdisciplinary researcher. She is the Publisher and Editor-in-Chief for Quantum Era Press, based in Santa Monica, California, which provides all prepress services to independent authors. She is also the Executive Director and a founder of the Sustainable Living Institute, a non-profit organization based in Santa Monica, California.

Her undergraduate studies were done at Stanford University, where she received a B.A. in political science. She completed a Master's degree in Clinical Psychology at the Western Institute for Social Research, in San Francisco, California.

After graduating with a B.A., she worked as an investigative journalist and was an editor/managing editor for various print publications. After receiving her Master's degree, she had a successful private practice as a psychotherapist for thirteen years, then quit to be able to do something different – first to pursue environmentalism, then to work in the Internet industry as editor for online publications. For the past fourteen years, as owner of Quantum Era Press, she has been helping other authors publish their own books.

Karen is also the author of *Garden of Light: Aligning with Your True Nature and Receiving Inner Guidance* (Warm Springs Press, revised 2016), and co-author of *How to Get Married After Forty: A Radical Approach to Finding and Keeping Your Mate* (Warm Springs Press, 1980, revised 2013, 2016). Her volume of poetry, entitled *Letting the Wind Blow,* has been published as an ebook (Warm Springs Press, 2016).